Mel Curtis

96868

CW00853391

# THE PIONEERING PRACTICE

## THE 9 KEY STRATEGIES
## FOR YOUR ACCOUNTING PRACTICE TO
## STAND OUT AND BUILD LUCRATIVE RELATIONSHIPS

AMANDA C. WATTS

The Pioneering Practice
First Published in 2018

This book is not intended to provide personalised legal, financial or investment advice. The author specifically disclaims any liability, loss or risk which is incurred as a consequence, directly or indirectly of the use and application of any of the content of this work.

Cover Design: Katie Bell
Author: Amanda C. Watts

All rights reserved. No part of this publication may be reproduced, distributed, or transmitted in any form or by any means, including photocopying, recording, or other electronic or mechanical methods, without the prior written permission of the author, except in the case of brief quotations embodied in reviews and certain other non-commercial uses permitted by copyright law.

For my Daddy – my inspiration

# CONTENTS

# FOREWORD

Amanda identifies one of the biggest opportunities facing accounting practices today. Leveraging technology to build relationships and provide outstanding service.

It is often proclaimed that accountants and bookkeepers are top of the list to be replaced by robots, however, the days of accountants are not numbered.

The accountant isn't dying. In fact, the pioneering accountant is actually thriving.

Today's accountant needs to develop specific skills and develop certain attributes to keep them relevant. As long as there is complexity involved with running a small business, there will be a place for accountants. Whilst much of the traditional work performed is being automated, there is an important human element to the relationship that a business owner has with their accountant. This relationship cannot be replicated by a robot.

In this book, The Pioneering Practice, Amanda has identified how marketing and sales can empower accounting practices to remain relevant and enable them to build strong relationships, reduce client churn and build trust.

This book clearly addresses the questions on many accountants mind. Should I niche my practice? How do I niche my practice? How do I use social media, and which platforms should I be using? Amanda then goes on to share one of the most powerful marketing platforms we have embraced at The Wow Company – events.

This book demonstrates the steps you need to scale up your firm and become a pioneering practice. The ideas detailed in each chapter walk you through a proven methodology which has a track record of success.

Every modern business, regardless of their size or age, needs a modern accountant who knows how to future-proof and grow a business. This book will show you how to ensure you understand your clients' needs, your own needs and how to leverage the tools and technology available, so you can continue to provide excellent service to your clients.

Approach this book with an open mind, and an attitude of learning a new skill and it will serve you, and your clients well.

This is a book I recommend to accountants who want to pioneer their way forward...

Here's to your success.

**Paul Bulpitt**
Founder of The Wow Company & Head Of Accounting Xero UK

x

*The Times They Are A-Changin'*
*Bob Dylan*

Once upon a time there was a profession that was essential to the running of a business. Not too long ago this profession was highly regarded, highly valued and a vital part of both a company and its success.

Those who worked in the profession were sought out for their expertise, respected by their clients, and referred and recommended on a regular basis. As a result, they were rewarded with a good income and a profitable business.

But times started to change. The profession was no longer as viable in the 21st century as it had been previously. The impact of technology meant that many tasks that could once only be done by these learned technicians had now been automated. Many of their former tasks had become commoditised.

At the same time, parts of the media and industry were rife with scaremongering. The profession was constantly being told that one day, and perhaps in the not-too-distant future, it could become obsolete.

However, not everyone believed this. Some, who I like to call pioneers, saw ways in which this new technology could be leveraged, and the opportunities that could be created to enable them to thrive in this new world.

Would it be simple? Probably not. Would it be worth it? Most definitely.

These pioneers made it their mission to disrupt their industry and challenge the status quo. To do so, they did things that were out of their comfort zone. They explored new ideas, and climbed huge mountains to reach the summit of success.

In short, they changed the way they ran their business. They attracted new opportunities. They became the lifeblood of other businesses. And they returned to being both highly valued and highly paid.

# INTRODUCTION

*The pessimist complains about the wind; the optimist
expects it to change; the realist adjusts the sails.*
William Arthur Ward

## WHY DO YOU RUN YOUR OWN PRACTICE?

When I ask clients why they became an accountant,
they often answer "I found it interesting and I was
good at it."

Those, however, that have made the leap and started
their own accountancy practice give me a different
answer: Freedom. The freedom to spend more time
with their family, friends and doing what they love,
outside accountancy, that is! Unfortunately, freedom
continues to elude most practice owners who, in
reality, work too hard, facing long hours for very little
return. And it's getting worse. As more and more
services are commoditised and profits are squeezed,
practices need more clients to make up for their
decrease in income. In addition, clients are less loyal
than they used to be. Freedom often feels as if it will
never come.

## TECHNOLOGY HAS CHANGED THE LANDSCAPE FOR EVER

The business world is experiencing more change and upheaval now than at any other point in its history. And advances in technology aren't just affecting our business life, they're also affecting our personal life. Such rapid developments mean that the way we talk, move and interact with people and the world today, would have been almost entirely alien to people even 30 years ago.

What's more, the changes won't be slowing down any time soon. In fact, they're getting faster and faster every day. And they haven't been brought about by war, famine or political upheaval, but by a phenomenon we've never seen before: the internet.

This phenomenon has levelled the playing field for accounting firms, both small and large. You no longer need deep pockets to market a business. All it takes is a click, a tweet or a video on YouTube and you can reach thousands of people around the world.

Most importantly, the fact that the internet can leverage our visibility offers huge opportunities. We can now compete not just against other accountants in our local town, but also against companies who offer slightly different, or related, services.

Disruptors in any industry start their business from an idea and grow it fast – often from their bedroom or parents' garage. It's now possible to run a multimillion-pound business working from a laptop whilst sitting in your underpants eating bacon sandwiches and drinking tea.

These changes have led to industries being disrupted by pioneering businesses, businesses that in turn are now inspiring others to disrupt, innovate and be more agile than ever. Everything has changed. Airbnb, Uber and Netflix are just a few examples that have already made (or are well on the way to making) expensive hotels, taxis and Blockbuster Video obsolete. And there's a lot we can learn from them.

Within the accounting profession, Xero and QuickBooks are replacing bookkeepers, while apps and other technology are halving the manual work accountants need to carry out. However, at the same time the apps, along with platforms such as Practice Ignition and MyFirmsApp, are enabling accounting practices to deliver excellence and, in doing so, to build customer loyalty, relationships and their reputation.

## WHEN BEING GOOD ISN'T GOOD ENOUGH

Once upon a time being good at your job was enough to secure you clients. There were enough clients for everyone and it was relatively easy to grow a healthy accounting practice. Accountants' technical training attracted clients as their skills made them vital to a business. They didn't need to stand out from the crowd. They just needed to be good at what they did.

But time has passed and accountants now need to think and act differently. Word of mouth and referrals alone are no longer enough to generate predictable revenue. The wrong clients can quickly drain practices of time and profit, while the right ones are hard to find.

That's why we need to be more visible, offer more value and present ourselves proactively as vital to businesses. Relationships are more important than ever, while trust is now built in a very different way.

## WHAT CHANGES DO YOU NEED TO MAKE?

*It's supposed to be hard, if it were easy everyone*
*would do it*
*Tom Hanks in A League of Their Own.*

25 years ago, in my first job, my responsibilities included the marketing of 27 magazines across a number of different industries. My job was to make them stand out on the crowded shelves of local newsagents. To do this, I relied on strong positioning in the marketplace, great content that people enjoyed reading, and an occasional free gift on the front of the magazine to persuade readers to buy it rather than one of its many competitors. The more magazines I sold, the more the sales department could charge for advertising. Marketing was a catalyst for sales.
These principles haven't changed. And they need to be applied to accounting practices that want to stand out, to be seen and valued.

However, the tools we use to maximise sales and leverage marketing have changed – dramatically. Many traditional marketing tools such as the Yellow Pages are now obsolete. The online readership of newspapers and magazines outstrips that of hard copies. Instagram allows people to become household names overnight, while others spend hours watching cat videos on YouTube.

We no longer "switch on the box" to watch the news. We scroll through Twitter, LinkedIn or Facebook to keep up to date. The small screen is now the screen we carry around in our pockets all day, every day.

Whereas we used to listen to the radio when drinking our morning tea, now each of us has our head down and is busy scrolling through social media, texts from friends or Snapchat.

Even if you have chosen not to live your life like this, most people do.

In a recent survey, Deloitte found that in the UK:

- 34 per cent of adults look at their smartphones within five minutes of waking and 55 per cent do so within 15 minutes.

- 78 per cent check their phones within the hour before they go to sleep, exposing themselves to the blue light which can impact on sleep quality.

- 34 per cent 'almost always', 'very often' or 'sometimes' use their smartphones when eating with family and friends at home.

- 11 per cent use their phones while crossing the road; and 53 per cent do so while walking.

In addition, amongst those aged 16-19, 66% check their phones after they've gone to bed, and 25% respond to any messages they've received. My question, then, is: which audience could become your clients in the next few years?

That's why you need to reach them – wherever they are. If they're scrolling through their phones for suppliers, relying on traditional referrals could kill your business.

## WHY READ THIS BOOK?

The principles that I'm going to share have enabled some in our profession to stand out, be seen and remembered. Those pioneering practices that have run with the ideas that I outline are disrupting the industry and reaping the rewards.

Below, I'll share the story of the two founders of an accounting practice who spotted a massive gap in the market and launched a business based on a very strong "why".

This "why" has propelled them into becoming the directors of a successful business with 40 employees, being seen as industry leaders and enjoying their life.

You'll also read about Gary, who almost ran his business into the ground (using a technique that most accounting practices think will get them quick wins, but which ultimately restricts growth) and about the sole practitioner who leads a team of eight, and who manages to be a niche celebrity without niching his practice!

You'll learn how to attract high-value clients and only work with those you enjoy working with.

You'll read about pioneering practices that will help you stand out in a commoditised market place. Practices that no longer rely on word-of-mouth referrals, but leverage marketing and offer predictable revenue.

I wrote this book with one mission in mind: to open you up to new ideas and to help you market your firm in a new way. I promise that if you make it your mission to understand, learn and action the concepts it offers, you too can become a pioneering practice and increase the time, money and freedom you have available.

## HOW IT WORKS

The Pioneering Practice is organised into three parts:

- **Engage**
- **Connect**
- **Convert**

Part one will help you build the visibility of your accounting practice. We'll look at why you do what you do, who you help, how you help them and the marketing platforms you need to engage with your audience.

Part two will see you ready to create and implement a strategy that builds your relationships and credibility. You'll learn how to attract educated buyers, to be seen as an authority in your field, and to earn the trust of your audience. You'll also learn how best to connect with leads.

Part three will show you the power of event marketing, how to run a pioneering marketing campaign and how to secure those all-important referrals. You'll also discover how to convert a lead into an evangelical client.

If you follow the book in order I promise it will work. If, however, you skip to implementing part three without working through parts one and two, you'll struggle. In fact, one of the main reasons some accounting firms claim that modern marketing doesn't work is because they do just that.

No matter how excited you are, I urge you to read the book through from beginning to end. Then, read it again – this time poised with your highlighter so that you don't miss the nuggets that explain why you need to be a pioneering practice.

Enjoy, and I look forward to hearing about your wins and breakthroughs. If you're ready to dive in, then turn the page now...

# Part 1
# ENGAGE

*Everything you do online leaves a digital footprint.*
*Your job is to create a footprint that others want to*
*follow, and to bring their friends with them.*
*Amanda C. Watts*

Apollo 11 was the spaceflight that landed the first two humans on the moon. Mission commander Neil Armstrong and pilot Buzz Aldrin landed the lunar module Eagle on 20 July, 1969. Armstrong was the first to step onto the moon, Buzz did so about 20 minutes later.

The landing was broadcast live on TV to a worldwide audience of around 600 million.

They became household names, and inspired others to follow in their footsteps.

Their epic voyage didn't come easily though. Much groundwork needed to be done first. Rockets needed building. Tanks needed fuelling. Systems needed testing and tweaking. Astronauts needed training.

Neither Neil nor Buzz decided to make that trip to the moon without forethought and planning. They made sure the foundations were in place first to ensure that the trip was a success.

They were also not the first to try to reach the moon. NASA had tried before, yet failed. However, these failures did not stop NASA from persisting. In fact, they inspired them to keep going.

The measuring and tweaking had taken place during previous missions. A turbo-pump gearbox malfunction scuppered the first try. Excessive vibration of the rocket scuppered the second. Premature second stage cut-off scuppered the third ... And so it went on. Each of these failures was a lesson. They were the vital foundation of launching a rocket into space.

Not only did the space rocket have to be fit to fly, so did the astronauts. They had to be both physically and mentally fit.

Whilst your accounting practice may not have quite as many moving parts as a spaceship, growing it still requires you to get the basics right if you want to achieve your goals.

Your body needs to be fit. Your mind needs to be fit. And your business foundations need to be in place and have been tested, measured and tweaked. Then, and only then, will you be ready to market your accounting practice.

The foundation work is where you need to do most of the heavy lifting. And the chances are that, till now, you haven't spent much time on this. Which is why you're probably either spending money on outsourcing your marketing, or are burying your head in the sand by relying on referrals. Today, we're going to fix that.

In part one, we'll cover positioning in the marketplace, building a brand and choosing the platforms to be visible on. Then we'll launch your spaceship.

# STRATEGY 1 - POSITIONING

*Positioning is not about being seen as different from your competition, it is about being seen as the only solution to your clients' problems.*
*Amanda C. Watts*

Most people realise that positioning means standing out from the crowd and differentiating yourself from your competition. However, less people realise that it's also about making sure you clearly position yourself as the solution to your clients' problems. That way you'll be the first person they think of when they need help.

The strongest positioning efforts are those that have a single focused message for a single target market. Once you achieve this positioning in the marketplace you cut through the noise, you get seen and you attract the right people to your practice.

Once you're firmly positioned in a particular audience's mind, you become what I call a niche celebrity. It's about being well known by a certain group of people, or famous for a certain solution.

The knock-on effects of this are credibility, new opportunities and new clients.

Just like a celebrity in traditional terms, you're looking to attract the right kind of attention from the right kind of audience. This is what niching does. It means you understand the difficulties that a certain kind of client faces and can provide a solution to overcome them.

## BEING A NICHE CELEBRITY

In some ways I have become an example of being a niche celebrity. I get asked to speak about my marketing ideas and strategies, people watch my videos, read my books and attend the events I organise.

I am not a celebrity like Brad Pitt or the Kardashians, but I am well known to my ideal clients. I have thousands of followers on Twitter and Facebook and when I go to events many people know who I am and already trust my expertise.

In other words, I'm a celebrity to a small niche of people and that's all it takes to have a successful business. My friend Matt is another niche celebrity. He specialises in helping IT companies with inbound marketing. His industry know, like, and trust him. He's regularly featured in blogposts, podcasts and has been interviewed on the BBC a few times.

Another niche celebrity is Alex. Alex is a dynamic, forward-thinking, tech-savvy accountant. She's never spent a penny on marketing but has still managed to create a niche celebrity status. She's asked to speak on podcasts. She wins awards. She represents suppliers from the accounting industry like Xero and Practice Ignition, and is highly respected, highly paid and loves running her practice!

Robert Frith is an accountant who lives in my local village. He, too, is a niche celebrity. He runs local events, has written a book and is well known to a few thousand people.

The aim isn't for you and your pioneering practice to be known by everyone and anyone, but by a particular group of people. This group is your audience, and you'll be the niche celebrity its members will want to follow.

To be a niche celebrity you need to have certain foundations in place:

- A clear positioning in the marketplace. This includes what you do and who you do it for.

- A strong marketing message that's easily understood and attracts your ideal audience.

- A personal brand that's known and trusted, and which presents you as an expert authority.

- And, finally, a stage – which we'll refer to as platforms. These platforms are where your audience can find and engage with you.

Primarily, positioning is "the place a brand occupies in the minds of its audience". But herein lies the problem. Most accounting practices are not in people's minds. At least not until they need help with payroll or year-end accounts. It's only when an audience needs help that they'll seek out a specialist or ask for a referral.

But, unless you've purposely positioned your accounting practice with either a specific audience or service, you won't be at the front of anyone's mind when it comes to referrals, nor will you be known as a specialist or a problem solver.

If this is the case, you'll most likely be a generalist.

This lack of positioning in a prospect's mind has a knock-on effect. When a prospect chooses to work with a generalist firm their purchase decision is often price-driven and the practice is not valued and respected as much as a niche firm. A generalist firm has more work to do building trust with a new client, and proving that they're an expert at what they do.

If you haven't positioned yourself in the marketplace, you'll have little choice but to be less picky about who you work with. In fact, you'll probably find that you work with clients who drive you nuts and drain your energy. I refer to such clients as vampire clients, as they suck the life out of you. And they don't just affect you at work. When you get home, thinking about them will also encroach on your time with your family.

Conversely, an expert can charge their worth. They've already built credibility and trust. Once you've positioned yourself as such, buyers won't quibble on price. They'll trust your advice and take on board your recommendations and actions. A great accounting client will do the necessary prep work and your life will become, dare I say, easier!

David Ogilvy, often referred to as the father of advertising, refers to positioning as two things: what a product does, and who it is for.

So the first step, before you even begin to think about marketing your practice, is to work on what you do, and who you help.

## NICHING YOUR PRACTICE

Without a clear process in mind, niching can seem hard – and scary. "How can I decide on a niche for my firm, when there are so many different people I can help?"

Some people worry that niching their accounting practice will limit their opportunities and slow growth. However, the opposite couldn't be more true.

The Wow Company has nearly 40 staff, and its niche is digital agencies looking for business growth. However, the company didn't start with this specific niche. Its founders built a general client base and focused on building systems and getting a great reputation; then their niche found them. They studied their clients. They worked out who they most enjoyed working with, and who they could make the biggest difference to. The founders, Paul Bulpitt and Peter Czapp, saw their digital agency clients were doing some cool stuff and that they could help them. So they created specific events for this niche. They wrote specific blogposts, and created a specific community that digital agencies could become part of.

Did they put all their eggs in this one basket? No.

They created what I call a "hunting niche". A specific niche at which they targeted much of their marketing. But they didn't turn away other clients. At first glance, in fact, their website looks fairly generic. It's only when you dig a bit deeper that you find their hunting niche.

They do, however, run their practice like a clubhouse. Let me explain.

## THE CLUBHOUSE RULE™

Imagine that a friend's invited you to play a round of golf at an exclusive club he's a member of. You've wanted to play at this club for a long time, but never managed to get an invite before. Today is your lucky day.

You arrive at reception and are asked for your name. The receptionist checks the VIP guest list, finds it, smiles and ushers you through to the clubhouse where you're met by your friend and other golf enthusiasts with whom you have much in common.

By this point you're feeling pretty good. You're excited and are anticipating a pretty awesome day filled with some great things.

This is how your clients should feel when they start working with your practice.

But if you're trying to be all things to all people, how can you recreate this experience for them? In short, you can't.

If you don't have a member of your team to vet clients before they work with you, anyone could enter your clubhouse. Now your clubhouse is neither seen as exclusive, nor valuable.

You only want to work with people who value what you offer. You only want to work with people who are your kind of people. Only then will you truly love your work and enjoy doing it. The knock-on effect is that it means you'll also do your best work, which in turn is great for your reputation.

And remember: who you hang out with matters. When I was a child my parents wanted me to be friends with a certain kind of person. They didn't want me to hang out with a bad crowd, with people who weren't good for me or for my reputation. At the time I thought how unfair this was, but in all honesty (and now that I am a parent myself) I totally understand. We are the company we keep. We need to choose our clients as wisely as we choose our friends.

In 2009, when I started my business, I worked with anyone who would pay me – no matter how little. Then I began to realise that this meant I was poor, frustrated and stressed much of the time. I didn't feel valued. I was selling myself to the lowest bidder. And those clients who paid the least generally ended up being the most demanding.

This way of working had to stop. And that's why I created the Clubhouse Rule.

I began to consider what it would mean to work with clients who I actually enjoyed working with and who valued my expertise. It was at this point that I decided only to work with a certain kind of person. I chose a niche based on ten key principles. I created my clubhouse.

Here are those ten principles, so that you can create your own clubhouse:

1. Which clients do you/your team like?
2. What's the revenue per year for each client?
3. What's the profit per year?
4. Do they drain your time/energy?
5. Do they refer you?
6. Do they respond to your emails/calls quickly?
7. Do they appreciate you?
8. Do they pay you on time?
9. Do they listen to you?
10. Do they provide required information on time?

Whilst these may not be the only principles for your particular requirements, they're a great place to start. They'll ensure that you're left with high-value, A-grade clients and a pretty cool clubhouse.

The knock-on effects will be increased productivity, profit and freedom for you, and a wonderful experience for your clients.

## NOW IS THE TIME TO BE A PIONEERING PRACTICE

I wouldn't have been able to write this book 30 years ago. 30 years ago you either had a lot of money to throw at expensive advertising or you were busy building your practice based on referrals. There was little chance of you becoming a niche celebrity. The tools weren't yet available.

30 years ago you still needed to be a generalist and to function as an accountant. Your firm had to fit within a category in the Yellow Pages, and it would do better if it was called AA Accountants than XYZ Accountants, simply because entries were listed alphabetically.

Until recently the big four and mid-tier firms controlled most of the industry, and the smaller local and boutique practices were run by people like my grandfather's financial adviser, Mr Baker, who gave me a sugary sticky jelly sweet whilst I waited patiently during their yearly meeting. There was no competing with the big boys.

Today it's different. Today it's a level playing field.

Yellow Pages are no more, and all accounting practices are equal in the eyes of Google. The good news is, you can dominate Google if you know how to play the Google Game™. And the more specialist you are, the easier it is to play.

The Hierarchy of Niching:

1. Micro-niching
2. Vertical niching
3. Horizontal niching
4. Generalist (i.e. no niching)

Niching is essential to being a Pioneering Practice. Below, I'll explain each niching strategy by asking – and answering – two questions: "What do you do?" and "Who do you help?"

**Generalist (no niche):** a generalist is all things to all people. Asked: "What do you do?", a generalist will answer: "I'm an accountant." Asked: "Who do you help?", they'll answer: "Anyone who needs accountancy work."

**Horizontal niche:** an accountant who has a horizontal niche is one who helps all people overcome a specific pain/problem. For example, asked: "What do you do?", they might answer: "I'm an accountant who specialises in tax." Asked: "Who do you do this for?", their response might be: "Anyone who is looking to minimise their tax payments."

Having a horizontal niche makes writing your marketing material so much easier. It also enables you to position yourself and your accounting firm as experts, because you can showcase how you have saved clients thousands and that you and your firm are master tax technicians.

**Vertical niche:** an accountant who has a vertical niche is more specific on who they help, rather than on the service they offer. When asked: "What do you do?", they'll respond: "I'm an accountant." But, when asked: "Who do you help?", they might answer: "I specialise in helping small tech start-ups."

A vertical niche starts to make marketing even easier. You'll understand the pains that small tech start-ups have and be able to market to them accordingly. You'll know where they hang out and what to say to them when you find them there. You'll also make it easy for your ideal client to self-select: "That's me! I'm a tech start-up and I'm looking for an accountant!"

**Micro-niche:** the holy grail of niching. This is when you're specific on both the problem (the service you offer) and the person or business you help. Asked: "What do you do?", you might answer: "I'm a tax specialist". Asked: "Who do you help?", you might answer: "I specialise in helping tech start-ups minimise their end-of-year tax payments, and maximise their profit."

If you were a tech start-up, which kind of accountant would you want to work with?

## CHOOSING YOUR NICHE

Just like The Wow Company, working out which clients you work most productively with is the best place to start. They're the ones you provide most value to, and most enjoy helping. If you can find the sweet spot of liking the client, their paying well, and you're being brilliant at helping them overcome their pains, then you've hit the jackpot.

When choosing a vertical or micro-niche you need to decide on an industry. A good niche is one that you can find in abundance on LinkedIn. To start your research, all you need is to search by industry sector. Whilst plumbers may not be hanging out on LinkedIn all day, there are over 17,000 of them listed in the UK alone. And over 100,000 throughout the world.

Other examples include interior designers, estate agents and hairdressers.

Remember: the clients you want, are the clients you'll be happy to invite into your clubhouse.

Examples of sectors within an industry include:

- accountants with a turnover of £150,000 per annum or more
- pub companies with three or more locations
- entrepreneurs who sell digital products
- haulage firms that want to sell their business within five years

Square Mile Accounting is a good example of a niche practice. Its core focus is pubs, bars and breweries. Its content is niche-specific. It writes for its ideal clients. It doesn't write about accounting in general.

One article that's well worth reading on the company's website is "A Step Tat-too Far?", which discusses whether tattoos are acceptable in the workplace. It's an interesting topic that works hard to attract their ideal clients to the website. It's an extremely pioneering way to leverage their niche marketing.

But there's no hard and fast rule. If you have multiple partners in your practice, you may decide to have multiple niches. If you don't want to niche your practice as a whole, then try hunting niches (where you niche your marketing activity, not your practice as a whole). That way you can still niche your marketing and stand out in the marketplace.

You may find this exercise helps get you started:

1. Make a list of possible niches/micro-niches you could work in.

2. Google them and see who pops up. If no one already has a clubhouse in a particular niche, then it's one you should consider.

Caveat: when choosing your niche it's important to ensure it has a market. Creating a phantom niche (one which only exists in your mind) means there may not be enough traction in that market. Make sure the niche you choose has enough people in it to enable your firm to grow.

# STRATEGY 2 - BRAND

There are bad brands, mediocre brands, good brands, consistent brands and then there are superstar brands. Superstar brands stand out from the mass of mediocre ones. They attract better staff, clients and opportunities.

Superstar brands generate more profits than other types of brand. They attract interest and are featured in blogs. They win awards and receive recognition for their value and contribution.

Superstar brands are never a flash in the pan. Year in, year out, they outperform all the other brands in their profession.

Yet, although all accounting firms have the same opportunities, the best that many achieve is a lacklustre presence and an underperforming accounting practice. And here's the thing: the path to having a superstar brand is brutally simple. Simple, mind you, but not easy.
So what's the secret that separates superstar brands from other brands? Two words: clarity and action.

Superstar brands are relentless when it comes to drilling down on their marketing message and how they show up in the marketplace. They're fanatical about how they look, how they sound and how they're perceived.

They don't believe that as an accounting practice they have to do what the profession has always done.

Partners don't outsource the responsibility of growing their practice.

They don't live in fear that someone might not like what they say or do.

They don't procrastinate and put off brand building "until tomorrow".

They show up even when they don't feel like showing up because they're driven and are a pioneering practice.

Superstar brands are never bland – they want to shake the status quo

## IN SEARCH OF THE EASY OPTION

"Pay £1,000 a month and get 15 prospect meetings booked for you", the telesales company tells you. "We'll do all the hard work. All you have to do is show up to the meetings."

If such companies didn't work, then they'd quickly go under. But what these "outsourcing" options do is allow you to abdicate control and attract the wrong kind of prospects to your accounting practice.

It's disappointing when accounting practices take the easy option. They somehow delude themselves that it's a sustainable way to grow an extraordinary practice. Then their partners complain endlessly about the quality of their clients and that they have too little time and too little money.

All the data that we've gathered over the years indicates that it's essential to build familiarity. Familiarity's such an important factor in getting prospects to engage with your brand. The more familiar your prospect is with you/your company brand, the more likely it is they'll accept a call from you and – ultimately – become your client.

- Each time you leave a voicemail and they hear both your name and your company's name, their familiarity with you increases.
- Each time someone visits your website, their familiarity with you increases.
- Each time you connect with someone on LinkedIn, their familiarity with you increases.
- Each time someone downloads one of your eBooks, their familiarity with you increases.
- Each time you meet someone at a conference, their familiarity with you increases.

However, if you don't have a strong brand, you won't become familiar. People will have to think hard to remember you – if they can at all. This lack of familiarity is why you receive so many objections to requests for your prospects' time.

Remember: Having a strong brand enables you to build familiarity. Familiarity builds relationships. Relationships build trust. Trust builds your practice.

## WHAT'S A BRAND?

Your brand isn't your logo, your business cards or the pop-up banner you take to networking events. Your brand is a combination of how you look, how you act and how you make people feel.

If your ideal prospect doesn't like the way you/your accounting practice looks, delivers or leaves them feeling, your accounting practice will struggle to attract and retain clients.

## THE PEOPLE'S VIEW

In 2017 I surveyed 500 people, asking them how they'd describe their accountant. Less than 20% could describe them at all, while the majority said they didn't really have a relationship with them. A few of the comments included words like "bland" and "boring".

As an accounting practice, you have a brand reputation already. In the same way that estate agents, car salesmen and lawyers all have a reputation. Because of this you're already labelled. Your job then is to change the way you're seen, and to change the reputation of the accounting profession and your label. And establishing a strong brand is the key way to change these perceptions.

You and I know that "bland" and "boring" aren't words that are applicable to accountants. Having worked with the profession for a number of years, and lived with a tax technician for most of my life, I know you're neither. But unfortunately not everyone else knows this. That's why it's imperative that we share your personality with the world and change the perception of the profession and of your accounting practice.

The good news is that through the new technology that's available to build familiarity with your practice you can also create a superstar brand that attracts loyal followers, clients and delivers an outstanding client experience. You can build your superstar brand at the same time as you're changing the way the profession as a whole is perceived.

## THE BRAND TRUST FACTOR™

What makes you trust a business?

Whenever you go to a seminar or similar event you'll often receive a feedback form asking you to grade the speaker, the content and the venue.
The speaker, the content and the venue are brands.

The speaker's brand is commonly known as a personal brand, the content is a product brand and the venue is a business brand.

If you grade the speaker, the content and the venue as 10/10, then you've probably experienced the Brand Trust Factor™. You'll have had an outstanding experience that either led you to buy the product or, at the very least, to recommend it to someone else.

However, if you graded the speaker as 7/10, even if you still graded the content and venue as 10/10, it's unlikely that you either bought or recommended the product. If you did, you're likely to have included a "but": "The content and venue were great, but the speaker was just OK."

The reduced score means that you weren't convinced by a key part of the brand. In other words, you didn't fully trust it.

A similar process takes place every time a prospect engages with your accounting practice too. That's why it's essential to craft your brand if you want to score 10/10.

Once a prospect has graded you 10/10, you'll be able to convert them into a client without having to quibble on price or value.

But to convert a prospect into a client three things need to happen:

1.  They need to trust **your accounting practice**.
2.  They need to trust the **services you offer**.
3.  They need to **trust you** (a partner or key person in your team).

However, most accounting practices don't focus on building their brand in such a way as to build trust. In fact, often no time or planning is put into building a purposeful brand at all.

Another important factor to note is that 70% of your Brand Trust Factor™ is built before a prospect even speaks to you or to someone else in your accounting practice. In other words, they've completed 70% of their journey as a buyer without you even noticing.

Your Brand Trust Factor™ starts being built as soon as a prospect finds you on Google, follows you on social media or watches your videos on YouTube. This is why building an online brand is so essential to your success.

In fact, before we go any further, I challenge you to see where you stand on the scorecard. If I were to Google you right now, for example, how much trust would be built for your brand before I even spoke to you? If I Googled you or your accounting practice, would you dominate the first couple of pages?

I wonder if you've heard the joke: "Where do you hide a dead body? On page two of Google." I hope this drives my point home.

## BUILDING YOUR BRAND TRUST FACTOR™

As mentioned, you need three strong brands to engage, connect and convert a prospect into a client. Each requires different strategies, and one is simpler and faster to build than the others.

## YOUR PRACTICE (BUSINESS) BRAND

Your accounting practice needs a strong brand presence that people identify with high quality, fantastic results, great customer service and an even better reputation. If your practice isn't recognised for these factors you'll attract the wrong sort of client and be driven down on price. In fact, because you're so desperate you'll take on any clients.

### Say goodbye to being "cheaper, faster, better"

For years, many in the profession have chased the holy grail of being cheaper, faster or better to attract clients. However, in today's world and with the current pace of innovation, being cheaper, faster or better is no longer enough. Your clients are savvy buyers who've researched the solution to their pains before speaking to your practice. (Remember: they've completed 70% of the buyer's journey before they connect with you.)

Clients are looking for an accounting practice that aligns with their values and that they feel an emotional connection with. In addition, consumers demand more from their suppliers and businesses than ever before. They're used to innovation and expect a trusted relationship.

That's why you need to focus on innovating faster than your competitors and on building trust with prospects and clients. So let's look at both in a little more detail.

Whether you create a new way of delivering your services, or a new product or package for your accounting services, innovation is key if you want to stand out from the crowd and build trust.

To give a first-hand example, my team and I created the Pioneering Practice programme in 2017. It offers a fresh way for accounting practices to approach marketing by combining ideas from traditional, modern and pioneering marketing techniques, as well as by tapping into other pioneering industries for break-through ideas. This innovative approach has led to our business and to those of our clients becoming more visible, vital and valued.

Or let me share the story of Blue Rocket Accounting who, on the surface, look like a traditional accounting practice.

However, once you dig a little deeper you'll discover they've created a strong customer relationship management system that's both innovative and pioneering. This has enabled them to provide a better experience for their clients, as well as to make the life of their teams easier. Blue Rocket Accounting has separated itself from the marketplace. It has the Brand Trust Factor™.

The other non-negotiable driver of trust is good relationships. Don't forget: It's eight times easier to keep an existing client than it is to get a new one. The accounting practice that owns its client relationships is the accounting practice that thrives.

Your clients, if they're happy, won't shop around for another accounting provider. They won't question what your practice does for them, continuously wonder if you're the best practice or quibble on price. A happy client is more likely to recommend your practice. If they notice an accountant online who's cheaper they won't be swayed. They'll be loyal because they trust your practice.

But the opposite is also true. Your clients could be building a relationship with another accountant right now. If you're not an accounting practice they're proud to use, if they don't have a strong relationship with you and your team, and if they only hear from you at year-end or when you want an invoice paid, you'll eventually lose them.

At this very moment, pioneering accountants will be speaking to your clients on LinkedIn, writing articles and recording videos that answer their questions, and holding events that will lure them away from your practice and towards their own. Unfortunately, you won't realise any of this until it's too late.

That's why, even if you already have a thriving accounting practice, you need to focus on building and keeping relationships. Sharing your insights, ideas and providing value will stop your clients from looking around.

If you Google Blue Rocket Accounting you'll see that they're busy sharing their insights in blogs and videos; that they have an interesting and fun social media presence, and that they run events. They attract new clients through building relationships, and they nurture their relationship with their current clients. If you're an accountant based in Kent, then Blue Rocket Accounting are likely to be on the radar of your client base. So it's your job to keep your clients happy unless, that is, you want to lose them to a pioneering practice.

That's why a strong business brand is so important.

## YOUR PRODUCT/SERVICE BRAND

Do you currently sell your accounting services one at a time? One of the accounting firms my father works with does. It offers a menu from which clients can buy options including bookkeeping, year-end accounts, payroll and quarterly VAT returns. But the list is a full side of A4 and, to a non-accountant, confusing. Using a list like this muddles the buyer and decreases your Brand Trust Factor™. Running your practice this way and lots of people do – can lead to your being seen as a jack-of-all-trades rather than someone able to solve a client's specific problem.

The way to overcome this muddle, and instil trust is to devise different packages that your client can choose from depending on their particular needs and situation.

Blu Sky Chartered Accountants understand that packaging services and offering a solution that overcomes their clients' pains builds the Brand Trust Factor™.

That's why they offer the choice of four different packages called Exceed, Prosper, Initiate and Secure.

They understand what their clients need at each stage of their business growth, and that they have a specific problem to which one of their packages can supply the solution. By understanding their clients pains and frustrations in their business, BluSky Chartered Accountants can prescribe the right package to help them. Rather than a smorgasbord, they offer a well-devised solution to their clients' key pains.

Because BluSky Chartered Accountants have a clear understanding of their ideal clients, they can create a packaged service tailored to their clients' needs. If you are a fast growing or mature business, their exceed package which provides a "virtual FD" service could be perfect for you.

BluSky would score 10/10 for the Trust Factor of their product brand. If you Googled the co-founder Jon Dudgeon you'll see he also scores 10/10 for both his business and personal brand. It's one of the reasons why the practice is having such successful growth and making such a strong brand impact.

iHorizon are another good example. They have three offerings depending on the stage of your business:

1. Financial Management (seed to series A)
2. Financial Controller (series A onwards)
3. Advisory (growth-support & exit)

Both iHorizon and BluSky Chartered Accountants understand that a prospect is looking for a complete solution. A packaged service that overcomes a prospect's problems instils confidence in their services and builds a high trust factor.

That's why you need a strong product brand.

## YOUR PERSONAL BRAND

If you're lucky enough to work for a well-known accounting practice, then getting clients will be easier. However, even the largest accounting firms understand the power of leveraging a personal brand.

The personal brand is my favourite, simply because it's the easiest way to create a big impact in a relatively short period of time. By focusing on providing value through content creation and being helpful, you can build a personal brand that gets known, liked and trusted in as little as three months.

Directly investing in improving the familiarity of your name, expertise and reputation will dramatically increase your ability to build your practice. And you can leverage technology something that's leaving a lot of firms scared to your advantage.

Whilst it's true that some technology developments have taken away opportunities for accounting practices, others have enabled you to create a bigger impact. In fact, they can help you to build a personal brand in a way that, in the past, only celebrities and the wealthy were able to.

Today, distributing content is easy. You can share your thoughts through your website, social media channels and podcasts. You can raise your personal profile quickly and at very little cost.

Yet there's another methodology so little used in personal branding that I truly believe that any partner or team member that embraces it will own their territory.

And that is Speaking.

From the moment you walk on to a stage or to the front of a room you're a celebrity. After you've given your talk, people will walk up to you. They'll ask you questions. They'll see you as an expert. They'll freely reveal their business issues to you and hand over their contact information.

## IF A 12-YEAR-OLD CAN, SO CAN YOU

Today, children in secondary school are already building a personal brand. Through the use of Instagram, Facebook and Snapchat it's possible for everyone to be a celebrity.

If you have a 12-year-old, chances are they're adding pictures to their Instagram account before they dash off to school. The food they eat, the clothes they wear, and who they hang out with is captured on camera and shared for the world to see. Their Instagram account is their personal brand.

We can't escape the fact that the world has changed.

Even if you've chosen to keep your personal life private, your children's social media accounts are probably followed by more people than those of your accounting practice.

Whether you've grown up with the explosion of technology and personal brands, or dread the thought of them, there's no doubt in my mind – or experience – that they're the answer to building great relationships and trust.

Take a look at Deloitte to see how they've embraced the power of the personal brand. They've put a face to all the partners within their departments, and purposely ensure that these partners build their credibility as influencers and experts. Deloitte understand that they need to leverage the people in their firm to build deeper relationships with clients and the Brand Trust Factor™.

Alex Falcon Huerta, founder of Soaring Falcon Accountancy, understands the importance of a strong personal brand, too. If you Google her name, her LinkedIn profile comes up. Then her accounting practice website. Then her Twitter feed and personal brand website. Then her videos on YouTube and her articles on AccountingWeb, Xero and Accountex. In fact, the first 10 pages are about her. So Google Alex Falcon Huerta if you want to see how you can raise your personal brand.

A strong personal brand will elevate your visibility, which in turn will engage more people to connect with you. This initial connection then builds into a relationship in which the trust factor grows and prospects are converted into clients.

Deloitte, BluSky and Alex all understand that running an accounting practice in the traditional way is no longer effective. They've had to innovate, build relationships and instil trust in a way that was incomprehensible just 15 years ago.

It's impossible for you and your accounting practice to be immune to the changes that have taken place. But I promise these changes aren't difficult to overcome. Once you have a strategy in place, you just need to work at it.

## THE GOOGLE GAME™

The Google Game™ is something you need to win if you want to be a pioneering practice. To win it, you need to be Google-able. This means that you need to ensure that you, your firm and information about you and your firm show up in all the major search engines and on social media. Whenever you create content, speak at events, maintain a social media presence or provide value to your audience, your name will show up. Unlike a traditional celebrity, with their name in lights, as a niche celebrity you need your name on Google.

Then, and only then, will you have a superstar brand.

EXERCISE

Open Google and type in "accountant" and your location or niche. Where does your firm rank? Have you made it into the top three of accounting practices listed in your local area or niche?

What do prospects find when they visit your website? Does it position your practice, your services and you as the go-to expert/niche celebrity?

Google your name. What comes up? If you are not happy with your answers to any of the above, what do you need to do to win The Google Game™? It would be good to write down your answers and refer back to them, tracking your marketing results as you implement the 9 key strategies.

# STRATEGY 3 - PLATFORM

*All the world's a stage*
*William Shakespeare*

Over four centuries later, Shakespeare's words are even more true.

Today, everyone can have their two minutes of fame. Whether we choose to do so on an actual stage, or through writing articles, recording videos or authoring a book, we can share our message with a large crowd, one hungry for our words.

In the previous chapters, I explained the importance of positioning and branding your accounting practice. I covered how to show up with a strong brand and who to show it to.

Now it's time to move on to the "where". In other words, to the platform. Where do you need to show up if you want your audience to find you? Which stage will best help you to share your message, entertain your audience and be seen as valuable?

## THE NEW STAGE

I don't have a talk show or a radio show. You won't have seen me on billboards or my name in lights in the West End. Yet, despite this, you're reading my book. My book then is a platform. It's the stage on which I get to share my script with you.

I have more than one platform. I have my websites, webinars, events, social media channels, speaking appointments, podcasts and TV and radio interviews. But this didn't happen overnight. I've built my platforms over time – just as you'll build yours.

Once upon a time consumers bought from you because your services were either in vogue or you had the best products. Those days are long gone, for the following reasons:

1. Competition has never been greater. When I Googled for a new videographer in the London area recently the results were overwhelming. There were over 2.6million of them. Similarly, "accountant in Surrey" returns more than 1.8million results. Then there's the fact that your competition's no longer just other accounting practices, but companies such as Xero, business coaches and online learning platforms as well.

2. People are more distracted than ever. With so many marketing messages bombarding us every day, your ten-year-old website won't make an impact. Consumers' attention is finite, and you're in direct competition with all those competitors I mentioned above.

Although this may feel discouraging at first, it's also an amazing opportunity if you think about it. Understanding the power of platform, and implementing a strong strategy around it, will enable you to cut through the noise of the millions of accounting practices lurking on Google.

## PLATFORMS PROVIDE VISIBILITY

Platform is another word for stage. In fact, it's a stage that elevates you above the crowd. Until recently, the only stage available to most people was somewhere like Speakers' Corner in Hyde Park, London. If you had something to say, you could stand on an upside-down milk crate or a stepladder. Your mission was to elevate your voice above the noise of the crowd so that you could share your message.

A modern platform is the same. Today, Speakers' Corner is your social media channels and the events that you run. Choose the right platforms – the ones where your niche audience hangs out – and you'll soon stand head and shoulders above your generalist competitors.

## PLATFORMS AMPLIFY YOUR MESSAGE

On the real Speakers' Corner, you'll need to shout if you want your message to be heard. No megaphones or microphones are allowed. If you want your message to reach beyond the park it simply isn't possible. You can only speak to those standing nearby.

Platforms such as Facebook, Twitter and LinkedIn, however, leverage the reach of your message. Done well, not only do they enable your voice to be heard above the noise, but also to reach further around the country and even the world. The only limits are the quality and consistency of your distribution; nothing more.

## PLATFORMS PROVIDE ENGAGEMENT

Modern platforms provide an unrivalled connection with your audience. Unlike a stage, from where you speak at your audience, modern platforms enable a two-way conversation. This engagement helps build those trusted relationships which in turn grow your community, clients, potential team members and joint venture opportunities.

## THE WORLD'S YOUR STAGE

Traditionally, one stage was enough for most celebrities. Brad Pitt's the star of movies, Sarah Brightman of stage musicals. But this "one-stage" approach won't work for businesses. You need multiple stages – platforms – for the following two reasons.

### 1. Building Your Platform On Sand.

Imagine your firm gets regular leads and clients through Facebook's advertising platform.

Now imagine Facebook suddenly decides it no longer accepts advertising. Whilst this may seem unlikely, they could easily block your firm – it's not unusual for a business to be put in Facebook "jail". If this happened your accounting practice lead-generation would nosedive overnight.

One of my clients, Gary, had something similar happen with his insurance company. He'd built up a nice business with a team of employees and a lead-generation strategy that was making him a multiple six-figure sum per year. His strategy relied on buying leads from – first – a single company, and then multiple leads from other companies. Although he was reliant on just this one strategy to get clients, his business thrived. He paid £15 per lead with a 30% conversion rate and £600 commission each time. It was easy.

But things started to change. By 2014, his profit had disappeared. The quality of leads had dramatically dipped, while their price had risen from £15 to £50, conversion had dipped from 30% to 10% and the average commission had gone down to £250.

The businesses he was buying leads from started to sell leads to his competitors, too. And the leads he bought had no trusted relationship with him – they weren't loyal, they just wanted the best deal they could get from him. The end result was he had to downsize his business and swore he would never buy leads again.

He set up a new business but, despite his vow, in 2016 he invested in lead-generation through the Google pay-per-click (PPC) platform. Again it seemed easy. He was paying £60 per lead but getting 4 times return on his investment. So, in January 2017, he decided to triple his PPC budget. Not long after, however, the cost increased from £60 to £168 per lead. In one month, he lost £12k.

He decided to try Facebook instead, but that didn't work and he lost even more money.

At that point Gary decided to change tactic. He saw that putting all his eggs in one basket and looking for easy lead-generation wasn't sustainable. He decided the solution was to choose a number of platforms, share insights and build trusted relationships rather than going for quick wins through paying for leads from a single source. Since then he's been creating videos, using Facebook and LinkedIn organically, written an Amazon best-seller and shows up on social media every day. His focus has been on raising his personal profile and building a superstar brand. As a result, by the beginning of April 2017 he was getting seven leads per week from his social media platforms and recommendations. Today, he's getting 19 and they're all coming to him organically from a number of different platforms. As he's provided more and more value to his ideal clients, he's seen a huge compound effect.

His platforms include his website as well as his accounts with YouTube, Facebook, Twitter, LinkedIn, Instagram and iTunes for his podcast. His leads cost nothing apart from the time he needs to invest to create valuable content and make sure he's visible. The knock-on effect is he no longer has to compete on price and is known as an authority and expert. He is visible, vital and valued.

This is the power of platform.

If currently you're only relying on referrals, pay-per-click advertising or telesales then you're building your practice on sand. You're relying on other people to bring you in clients, rather than creating a strong Brand Trust Factor™ and having predictable revenue.

## 2. No Two Prospects Are The Same.

The second reason you shouldn't put all your eggs in one basket is because no two prospects are the same. Each consumer will take a different amount of time and a different route along their buyer's journey.

That's why the platforms you choose shouldn't be decided by you or your accounting practice, but by your ideal clients. The choice of platforms is endless – and forever changing – so first decide on your strategy and tactics for engaging clients and only then choose your platforms.

To help, I'll run through some of the most important tactics now.

## SEEDS, NETS AND SPEARS

Have you heard of Aaron Ross? He built the outbound sales team at Salesforce. In his book, Predictable Revenue, he breaks down marketing activity into three very distinct and clear tactics: seeds, nets and spears. Over the past few years I've studied his concept and adapted it for accounting practices. The adapted concept yields tremendous results – every practice that adopts it sees impressive growth of client acquisition, client value and reputation.

Let me explain how it works, and the three marketing tactics your accounting practice needs to understand.

**Seeds – Word of Mouth:** this is how practices traditionally grew over the years. They used leads from campaigns based on word of mouth and relationship building. They sowed their seeds when networking and maximising referrals from current clients. It's still a highly valuable tactic.

**Nets – Inbound Marketing:** this is how pioneering practices are starting to grow their practice. They attract leads from one-to-many marketing campaigns. Examples include SEO, social media, webinars, eBooks and blogging.

**Spears – Outbound Sales:** these are leads obtained by direct prospecting, carried out through telesales, direct mail or direct LinkedIn messaging.

By optimising all three of these pipeline generators, you'll keep lead-generation high, drive sales growth and set your accounting practice up to thrive.

So let's look at them in more depth.

## SEEDS

Seeds are leads created through word of mouth, primarily from relationships built up over time, or as referrals from happy clients. As every accounting practice knows, seeds are the best leads you can generate. If they're generated by A-grade high-value clients, the chances are you'll be referred more A-grade, high-value clients. As the saying has it: birds of a feather flock together.

The Pros:

- Seed leads are highly profitable.
- You can on-board them super quickly.
- The number your practice receives is impacted by the experience you deliver to clients, and how often you ask for referrals and follow-up.

The Cons:

- Seed leads/clients can be difficult to gestate and need a lot of nurturing.
- They're often associated with relationships with the partners of a practice, so can be unscalable.

TIP: To grow your seeds you need to nurture clients, give them a great experience and focus on your influence network. You can do this through email marketing, by putting on events and by sharing your expertise. You'll never maximise the number of seeds you grow by providing a commoditised service. You need to provide a full and remarkable solution if you want to benefit from referrals.

## NETS

Nets are leads that you obtain through inbound marketing, for example through social media, blogging, video, webinars and events. Remember, you're casting your net wide with content, so it's about quantity as well as quality.

The Pros:

- Inbound marketing campaigns are scalable and can gain momentum fast.
- Leads come to you already interested in your firm and open to buying.
- As 70% of the buying decision is made before a prospect even speaks to you, leads from net marketing can become clients with ease.

The Cons:

- Unless you niche your audience, the information in your net will land on deaf ears.
- If that happens, lead generation will be slow, you won't be perceived as valuable or as a vital asset.
- You could end up taking on clients that aren't ideal, and your time, money and freedom will be squeezed.

TIP: It's essential to have a strategy behind your inbound marketing programme. You need to know who your ideal client is, and to understand their fears, frustrations, wants and aspirations. Then you need to be consistent. You also need to capture people's contact details once you've gathered them in your net. Not all prospects are ready to buy immediately. The benefit of harvesting contact details is that you can continue to nurture prospects with a keep-in-touch programme of email marketing, webinars and events etc.

## SPEARS

Spears are leads that your sales team or telesales company have reached out to directly. Spears are specific, targeted and should focus on quality over quantity.

Spears can only be part of your sales campaign if you know who your ideal client is and you can contact them directly. Spear marketing is fruitless if you're a generalist firm. I've seen clients pay thousands of pounds a month for telesales only to obtain poor clients who don't value their expertise. Don't fall into this generalist trap.

The Pros:

- If you can obtain a list of the specific audience you want to target, it becomes a numbers game. If you have a strong offer/message and have de-commoditised your practice all you have to do is pick up the phone or send a direct mail.
- LinkedIn is a great platform for spear marketing. After a few calls you'll know what to say to prospects and will be able to generate predictable revenue.

The Cons:

- If you have a small team it may not be profitable – if your sales team outweighs your technicians your costs will be too high.
- If you provide a low-priced service again it won't be scalable. You need to be clear on your tolerable lead-acquisition cost.

TIP: Use spear sales as part of your overall strategy. For example, create a net such as hosting an event in your town and then use spear marketing to fill it. Directly contacting your ideal audience to invite them will ensure that the right people – rather than tyre kickers or vampire clients – are in the room.

All three marketing tactics are complementary:

- Seeds provide quality leads as long as they come from quality clients and referrers. But they don't generate enough predictable revenue or enable you to scale.

- Nets are great leads but they take longer to gestate and only work when you target a specific audience.

- Spears provide quality over quantity and help to balance out nets and seeds.

By building a marketing strategy that incorporates a mixture of seeds, nets and spears your practice will receive a steady flow of leads. Most importantly, prospects will come to you, stay with you and refer you because they trust you, your firm and your services.

So, now your tactics are in place, how do you choose your platforms? Especially when there's such a plethora – both paid and organic – on offer. But, while I understand how daunting choosing can be, I hope you appreciate by now that burying your head in the sand and claiming you'll build your practice through referral marketing isn't the answer if you want to grow your practice.

I also realise that, just as you get your head around one platform, a new one (or an updated edition) is brought out and you have to start all over again. But that's why it's so important to understand your target audience and to know which platforms they use on a daily basis. That way you won't waste time on the wrong platforms. Instead, you'll maximise returns by being on the correct platforms and using the right tactics for your audience.

## WHERE DOES YOUR AUDIENCE HANG OUT?

Just like a stage, a platform is there to make it easy for your audience to connect with you. But if your platform is in the wrong part of town, instead of a full house you'll put on a show that no one comes to watch.

If your ideal clients are plumbers, then there's little point in local networking groups that allow you to reach one a week. You need to find a platform where plumbers hang out regularly, whether it's Google, Facebook or at events.

For example, one of our clients, Dan, runs an accounting practice that targets tradespeople such as plumbers and electricians. To do so, he's created specific landing pages for each of his trade niches. When a plumber visits his website they're directed to a specific page which offers a free download: "The Five Biggest Problems Stopping Plumbers From Having A Profitable Business". To download it, visitors must input their email address – which gives Dan the opportunity to market to them in the future.

The fact that Dan targets tradespeople means that by tailoring his advertising to them on Facebook and Google he can guide them to a specific landing page. Alternatively, he could send out a direct mailshot, call them or hold an event and invite only plumbers. By understanding his audience he knows which platforms will work and which – such as networking – would be a waste of time.

Raffingers are also a great example of a pioneering practice. In 2016 they rebranded from Raffingers Stuart to Raffingers and, along with a brand revamp, they updated their entire image to coincide with the rapid changes in the accounting industry.

One thing that really stands out for me is that they have chosen to use their website as the hub of all their marketing. From their website, they share their blogs and articles, have video testimonials to showcase their expertise and list events that are available for their audience to join if they so wish.

Raffingers are active every day on Twitter, Facebook and LinkedIn, and their team are actively engaging with their audience across these mediums.

But it is not just what you can see online that enables them to be a top 100 firm. They also ensure that they nurture their leads through email marketing and then, once they get a new client, they ensure that they deliver an exceptional customer experience. All of this activity enables them to be seen as a vital and valued accounting practice.

Once you've decided on your ideal audience, and have developed a strong message, it's time to choose a platform or two to test the water.

To get you started here are a few online options – but remember, the list may date quickly.

**WordPress (websites):** An excellent platform on which to build your authority, showcase your expertise and educate your prospects and clients.

**Facebook:** The world's biggest social network is used all over the world by all ages. And I promise it's not just somewhere they watch cat videos! You can pay to reach your target audience, and drive people to your website, blogs, events and webinars.

**Twitter:** A micro-blogging site where you can follow people and they can follow you back. You can share your blogs, thoughts, ideas and, at the time of writing, it's a great place to connect with journalists and be seen by influencers.

**LinkedIn:** The biggest directory of professionals out there and one that's virtually untapped by accountants. Opportunities abound to engage and connect with your ideal client.

**Instagram:** Not for the fainthearted but, although it currently requires a very strong strategy, accountants focusing on Instagram to generate leads are yielding good results. So if your ideal client hangs out on Instagram then it's time to take pictures of your team, post inspiring quotes and photograph your lunch.

**YouTube:** You can post videos that include your ideas, your marketing message and an interview or two. If you can get yourself invited on to a podcast, you can upload the audio, too.

**SlideShare:** Due to its high Google ranking, it's a great place to upload those PowerPoint presentations that've been gathering dust on your hard drive.

There are also various offline platforms you can consider.

**Industry-specific conferences:** Find out which conferences your ideal clients go to, then either get yourself invited as a speaker or – failing that – as a delegate.

**Events:** Can you exhibit at the events your ideal clients visit? If your ideal client is a restaurant, for example, should you exhibit at the Restaurant Show?

**Magazines:** What magazines do your ideal clients read? Could you become a regular contributor to them?

**Local newspapers:** Could you write a column in one to share your expertise? It was grassroots marketing like this that earned me the title of "Social Media Queen" when I lived in Salisbury. I leveraged traditional media outlets such as my local radio and regional newspaper, using offline marketing to promote my online marketing.

**Direct mail:** If you know who your ideal client is and can access their business address, then you should definitely be using direct mail. A letter in the post, followed by a call a week later, is a great example of spear marketing. Your results will be even more fruitful if you use direct mail and phone calls to drive people to an event which showcases your expertise. (We'll come back to this in part three.)

**Networking:** If your clients are hanging out at local networking events then organisations such as BNI (Business Network International) and 4Networking may be worth considering. But be wary: the quality of leads can be mixed.

**Referral marketing:** I couldn't end the list without including the most traditional way to find clients. However, if you do decide to use it to generate leads, then make sure you have a purposeful referral outreach strategy in place first – one which preferably includes clients and influencers in your niche.

*Remember:* Your platform is your stage. It's where you'll share value, entertain your audience, wow them with your knowledge and expertise and leave them so enthralled by your narrative that they'll want more from you.

If, however, you're still trying to be all things to all people you won't attract many fans. Don't forget that a niche or specialism lets you cut through the noise, stand out and be heard.

So, now that you understand how to engage an audience, let's start connecting and building relationships.

EXERCISE

Interview a few companies/people in your ideal niche to learn where they hang out.

Choose two platforms from the list and make sure you're highly visible on them.

# Part 2
# CONNECT

## BUILDING RELATIONSHIPS AND CREDIBILITY

Human beings are naturally social. We crave connection and positive interactions just as much as we crave food and water. Achieving them, however, depends on our ability to build relationships.

The relationships we crave aren't just with our family, friends or team members. We also crave relationships with our suppliers, our clients, and our peers. A strong relationship equates to trust. A poor relationship equates to reticence and caution. If we have a good relationship with someone we're loyal and caring. If we don't, then it's a relationship we want to leave.

## RELATIONSHIPS FIRST, SALES SECOND™

Relationship building doesn't happen overnight. I once gave a talk at Accountex titled "Please Will You Marry Me, Mr Accountant". It was an ironic look at how firms try to get their audience to buy from them without building the relationship and trust that is needed first. I reminded them of the golden rule: Relationships first, sales second.

Here are the three main characteristics that define a good client/accountant relationship:

- **TRUST**: The pinnacle of every good relationship. Once your client trusts you, you form a powerful bond that allows you to communicate more effectively. You also don't have to waste time worrying about them leaving you.

- **MUTUAL RESPECT:** When your clients respect you and your work they value your ideas and suggestions. Together you will develop better solutions based on your insights, wisdom and creativity.

- **OPEN COMMUNICATION:** We communicate through emails, telephone calls and meetings. The better you communicate with prospects and clients, the richer your relationship with them will be. All good relationships depend on open, honest communication.

Understanding how to build relationships is important. The way in which trust, respect and good communication are formed today is very different from 10 years ago.

Two fundamental shifts have taken place:

1. Clients' buying patterns have gone through a monumental change.

2. Whereas sales used to be the primary force in growing a practice, now it's marketing. As a result, the lines between the two have become blurred.

Let me explain by reminding you – at the risk of repeating myself, but it's crucial you recognise how it works across all your marketing activities – that 70% of trust is built before you even speak to a prospect.

In other words, before a prospect calls they've pretty much decided if they're going to buy from you or not. By carrying out their due diligence, they've already decided whether you're credible or not and have formed an opinion on your value.

As an accountant, you'll quickly realise that leaves only 30% of the relationship-building in your hands.

So what does this mean in practice?

If, in the year 2000, the percentage of the pre-conversation buying decision was as low as 0-30%, will this dramatic increase continue? In a few years, will 80%, 90% or even 100% of the buying decision be made without speaking to your sales team?

Such questions lead us on to the second shift. If you wanted to grow your practice a few years ago, you'd have invested in sales above all else. Likewise, if you were short on cash, marketing would be the first to go.

Sales used to be the driver and marketing used to be the expense. But that's no longer the case. The lines have become blurred and marketing is yielding greater success than ever before. Why? Because marketing builds relationships.

The accounting practices that are thriving are the ones that are breaking the rules and pioneering new ways to build relationships.

Zappos broke the rules when they allowed customers to ship shoes back to them at no cost. By removing a barrier that might stop people from buying, Zappos built trust. At the time their competitors laughed at them, today they all follow suit.

Netflix broke the rules when they allowed customers to watch films online rather than having to go to a shop to rent them. They respected their clients' time, and in return reaped the rewards. Blockbusters, who turned a blind eye to what Netflix were doing, no longer exist.

The way business is done has changed. Your consumer knows what they need from you, and if you don't deliver it they'll move on to someone who will.

So will you approach this chapter in the way that Blockbusters did the advent of Netflix? Or will you approach it with an open mind and consider how you might apply what you learn to your firm?

## FIXED MINDSET OR GROWTH MINDSET?

There are two types of accounting practice. Ones who say: "Sure, I can see how that would work."; "Yeah, I think we can apply that to our practice."; or "That'll really help change the way our industry is perceived."

This is what I refer to as having a growth mindset.

Then there's the other kind. The ones who say: "That's not applicable to our industry."; "No way, I'm not doing that. Our clients are different from other clients."; or "That's not how people buy accounting services."

This is what I refer to as having a fixed mindset.

Every time I give a talk to a group of accountants and ask who believes that their practice is different, every single one of them raises their hand.

That's because, as psychology teaches us, we all want to feel special, and being different means we're special. However, people don't buy from "different" businesses; they buy from trusted ones.

They have to have trust in your practice, in your services and in you. The businesses that have succeeded using the methodology outlined in this book have all focused on building relationships and trust.

The following pages will show you how to build on the foundations you've already established through positioning your firm, building your brand and choosing your platforms.

# STRATEGY 4 - EDUCATE

While I was carrying out research for this book I came across a shocking statistic. According to the Edelman Trust Barometer, only 8% of people trust what companies say about themselves.

In other words, when our websites say: "We really care about our customers and are proud of our customer service." Prospects read: "That's what they all say to begin with. Once they've got my business they'll ignore me."

Or, when our websites say: "We offer a unique approach to helping you with your accounts." Prospects read: "Sure, as does every other accounting practice."

I even found one firm who wrote: "We endeavour to provide a first-class service." "Endeavour"? You can already imagine prospects thinking: "Well, if you only endeavour to do it, I think I'll choose an accountant who promises it instead."

Unfortunately for this firm, they probably failed to achieve the trust of even 8% of people.

It's a serious problem: 92% of the time that you talk about your accounting practice you're not believed. And the more you talk about it, the more unbelievable you become.

The best way to build trust then is to be there when someone needs you. Consistently. The more you help them, the more they'll trust you. And the best way to achieve this is through education-based marketing.

## GOOGLE HAS ALL THE ANSWERS

It doesn't matter what you're looking for, if you type a question into Google it will give you an answer:

- How do I...?
- What's the best way to...?
- What's the statistic for...?
- What are the testimonials like for xyz company...?

Every day, people are searching for solutions to their problems. They ask Google and people on social media for help – and they're not picky about who responds.

If someone's asking a question about accounting, you need to be the one who answers.

The fact that very few firms do so is good news if you're a pioneering accountant. It means you can build trust by being the one who does.

## WHAT IS EDUCATION-BASED MARKETING?

Education-based marketing is the sharing of knowledge with the purpose of building trust. It helps you establish credibility with your audience through educational messages. Today's consumer lives in a highly digital and instantly gratifying environment. They only buy on their terms and according to their timetable.

For them to trust you, they need to be assured that they're dealing with the right accounting practice. One that keeps their best interests in mind.

Education-based marketing is the opposite of traditional marketing, which is based on selling rather than relationship building.

Audiences have grown tired of traditional marketing. However, if you share important facts and information that helps them to make a decision, they'll listen.

## HOW CLIENTS BUY

Every client that decides to work with your accounting practice will have gone through the same three-step education process.

If you're the one to take them through this process, then your practice will get their business.

## THE TRAFFIC LIGHT METHOD™

I developed this three-step process to build relationships and trust with your audience after spending years analysing content that converted prospects to clients (rather than content that simply created additional noise in an already busy world).

The Traffic Light Method™ will change the way you approach your education-based marketing and ensure that you reap the rewards for your efforts.

The Traffic Light Method™ takes two things into account that every prospect needs to decide whether yours is the right accounting practice for them: time and information.

Time, however, is something you have little control over. A prospect will only buy when the time is right for them.

## 97% OF PROSPECTS DON'T BUY IMMEDIATELY

When people are searching for answers to a problem only 3% are ready to buy immediately. 7% are ready to buy within three months and 40% within four months to two years. The remaining 50%, however, will never buy – someone in their family might be an accountant, or they might want to solve the problem themselves.

Knowledge is power, and these are powerful statistics to understand the impact of. You need to do certain things if you want to maximise conversion of prospects. Taking control of the situation by providing as much information as possible to a prospect, whilst also condensing their timeline, is a task that pioneering accountants need to embrace.

## TAKE CONTROL

Unfortunately, until now most accounting firms have failed to carry out education-based marketing. They haven't provided the right information or, worse still, they haven't provided any information at all to prospects looking for answers. This instantly kills the chance to build trust.

If you Google: "How do I increase profits in my business?", business coaches and consultants – rather than accounting practices – will show up. Yet it's accountants who are the experts in this area.

Or, how about if you Google: "Why do I have poor cash flow?". Yep, you guessed it. Not a single accountant shows up on the first results page (which most people never read beyond).

*The best time to start education-based marketing was ten years ago; the second-best time is now.*
*Amanda C. Watts*

While it's true that the best time for you to start education-based marketing was a few years ago, it's not too late. Especially with the Traffic Light Method™ to help ensure that your content marketing is of value and can cut through the hubbub online.

The Traffic Light Method™ consists of three stages: red, amber and green. Each has different actions which will help move prospects from being unaware of their problem, through being aware and looking for answers to, finally, taking action and choosing a supplier.

As you guide a prospect through each of these stages you'll build credibility, relationships and trust.

If you skip a stage, however, chances are you'll end up competing on price as you won't have built the trust you need to be seen as vital and valued.

## STAGE 1: RED – AWARENESS

If you can articulate your prospects' pain better than they can articulate it themselves, you gain the right to help them overcome that pain. – Taki Moore

A prospect at the red stage doesn't know they have a problem. You do – as they fit your ideal client persona – but, right now, they don't.

When your prospect's stuck at red it's your job to educate them. You need to highlight the pain they're feeling but can't quite pinpoint.

At this stage, never talk about you or your accounting practice. Instead, highlight what they're going through and reassure them that there's a solution.

## STAGE 2: AMBER – CONSIDERATION

A prospect stuck on amber knows they have a problem and what this problem is. However, they want to know more about it. During this stage show them they're not alone in their pain, reassure them that the problem is normal and then educate them on how to fix it.

Prospects at this stage want information to help them understand their problem and its solutions. They'll keep researching until they have enough information to allow them to move on to the next stage.

At this stage, educate them on the available solutions and demonstrate your expertise through the quality of your insights and content.

## STAGE 3: GREEN – DECISION

A prospect at the green stage is ready to buy. They know what their pain is, understand why they have it and are now looking for someone to help them get rid of it.

However, to maximise your Brand Trust Factor™, prospects need two things:

- To know what makes your accounting practice different from other practices.

- Proof that you and your firm can help them to solve their problem.

By this stage you need to have ensured that you have strong positioning in the marketplace, are able to offer numerous case studies and testimonials to prove your solution works, and have created a brochure to solidify your offering.

## WHAT KIND OF CONTENT SHOULD YOU CREATE?

This is often the biggest stumbling block when people first approach education-based marketing. The first step in creating great content is to understand your ideal clients "hot buttons".

Hot buttons are things that people lie awake at night worrying about, or spend hours dreaming of achieving. They require "away-from" or "towards" marketing. Away-from marketing helps people to move away from their problems and frustrations, while towards marketing helps them move towards their wants and aspirations.

Although towards marketing may seem to offer a nicer approach, away-from marketing can have a bigger impact. But you won't know which is best for your audience until you fully understand them.

So, for now, focus on understanding the four hot buttons:

- Fears
- Frustrations
- Wants
- Aspirations.

How might these look for your audience?

- I fear that my business isn't making enough profit.

- I'm frustrated that I don't have enough time to work on my finances.

- I want someone to rescue me and make it simple.

- I aspire to having a highly profitable business and more freedom.

Once you understand these four hot buttons, you can use education-based marketing to help prospects overcome them.

For example, in response to: "I fear that my (plumbing) business isn't making enough profit", this is the kind of content you could create for each stage.

**Red:** Write an Ebook on "10 Reasons your Plumbing Business is Leaking Profit."

**Amber:** Write a blogpost on "How to maximise the profit in your plumbing business and minimise your tax."

**Green:** Write a case study on "How XYZ plumbers worked with ABC accountants to increase their profits by 10% in one year."

## WHAT ARE THE DIFFERENT WAYS YOU CAN PRODUCE CONTENT?

Different consumers like to consume different kinds of content. Some like to watch videos or read blogs, while others appreciate the option to multitask when they're consuming content (for example listening to a podcast whilst driving). Similarly, some people prefer to go to live events, whilst others are so busy that this would never work for them. Instead, the latter group need to be able to access information in a way that fits into their lives as they juggle childcare or stressful jobs.

That's why you need to meet your audience where they choose, rather than where's most convenient for you. And remember: the more mediums you use, the more options your audience will have and the higher your chances of building more relationships.

Here are a few suggestions to get you started:

**Podcasts:** cheap to create, audio podcasts can reach thousands of people very quickly with tips to help them grow their business and sort out their finances.

**Videos:** a great medium for building trust. People buy from people, and in a video you're there for the world to see.

**Articles/Blogposts:** people short of time need to skim-read information and short articles and blogs allow them to do this.

**Books:** by showing your credibility, books enable you to educate and build a relationship with your readers.

**Webinars:** a mixture of video and audio (you can choose whether to show your face or not), PowerPoint webinars are a highly effective tool to educate your market.

**Events:** running an event automatically positions you as an expert. We invariably trust the person at the front of the room and believe they have the answers we're looking for.

## IT'S TIME TO THINK LIKE A MEDIA COMPANY

A while ago, on my way home from a meeting in London, I was reading the Evening Standard. Although it wasn't an action I'd set out to take, the vendor had asked if I'd like a copy as I walked past.

By chance he put some information in front of me and, as I had no other plans for my train journey, I chose to read it.

In fact, because my journey lasted 30 minutes and my phone battery had died, the newspaper had my undivided attention.

So why am I sharing this with you? Because, first, I wasn't actively looking for a newspaper; second, I was given the opportunity to read the paper, so I did; and third, because I did, I learnt some information and came across some new ideas.

This is the lesson about education-based marketing that I want to share. If you create content, people will read it. Even if they hadn't previously planned on doing so. You just need to get their attention.

That's why you need to think of your accounting practice as a media company. Because of the way information is now consumed and distributed, these days you're little different from a newspaper publisher, radio DJ or TV presenter.

Embracing this idea can transform your practice.

I'll run through today's equivalents of traditional media channels.

**Traditional:** newspapers. **Today:** articles on LinkedIn, blogs on your website, guest blogging. **Distributed through:** email marketing, Facebook advertising and organic social media.

**Traditional:** radio. **Today:** podcasts. **Distributed through:** iTunes, email and social media.

**Traditional:** television. **Today:** YouTube, Facebook Live, and LinkedIn videos. **Distributed through:** email marketing, social media, LinkedIn groups and your websites.

The traditional way to bring your accounting firm to an audience's attention was through the Yellow Pages, direct mail, leaflet drops or parish magazines. Whilst I'm still a fan of the last three, you also need to be found online.

Online platforms are the stage where your audience is waiting.

It's as simple as that.

Remember: I wasn't actively looking for a newspaper. I was rushing past a vendor and he gave me one to read. This is how we stumble across information now.

## HOW WE FIND INFORMATION ONLINE

We're scrolling our LinkedIn timeline, when we stumble across an article that catches our eye (or hits a hot button) and makes us want to read it.

We're skimming our Facebook feed when up pops an advert which reminds us of something we were searching for a few weeks ago, but forgot about. We hop over to Amazon and buy it.

We're chatting to our friends on Twitter, see an interesting article, click through to read it and the next thing we know an hour's gone by.

Hannah Xu runs an accounting practice for doctors who want to build their wealth and reduce their tax burden. She's been an accountant for eight years and has run her own practice for four. She has two apprentices and an admin team to support her.

Her platforms are speaking at events, LinkedIn and Facebook. She's also starting to use Instagram. She spends 4-5 hours per week marketing on social media. She educates her clients through video and, on Wednesday nights, she hosts a live stream on Facebook answering clients' and prospects' questions.

She also runs a Facebook group to which she adds clients to further improve the experience she can offer them and to add value. If someone asks her a question she can simply point them to a video she's already created on YouTube to answer it.

She uses the methodology of the Traffic Light Method™ to engage with prospects and to then connect and build relationships with them. Her dream is to create a lifestyle accounting practice, one where she has a small team and one which allows her to be flexible.

Through leveraging technology to add value, educating her audience and building authority as a niche celebrity, she's well on her way to achieving this.

**OVER TO YOU!**

Remember:

Be there when someone needs help – whether they already know they do or not.

Create content that'll disrupt their day and illuminate their problem. Show them WHAT their problem is.

Create content that helps them understand how to overcome their problem. Show them HOW to do this.

Create content that convinces them why they should choose your accounting practice. Show them WHO's the answer to their problems.

EXERCISE

Speak to your clients to find out their fears, frustrations, wants and aspirations.

Create three pieces of appropriate content for each stage of the Traffic Light Method™.

# STRATEGY 5 - AUTHORITY

Leaders, quite rightly, are the heroes of the business world. They motivate us to go to places and to do things that otherwise we'd never consider or believe possible. They change industries, organisations and produce memorable work.

Good leadership is the most important advantage an accounting practice can have. But sometimes, in our attempt to master the skills of being a leader, we lose sight of two of the most crucial attributes: visibly exceptional talent and the ability to attract followers.

When these two key skills meet, the leader is seen as an authority.

Leaders aren't focused on maintaining the status quo. They're focused on doing whatever's necessary to ensure growth and profitability in the future, which is not always the easiest path to follow.

However, becoming an authority doesn't just land in your lap. You need to make it happen.

The key lies in knowing what you're talking about and in being able to express it well.

In the land of the blind, the one-eyed man is king. – Genesis Rabba

To lead and be seen as an authority, you may think you need to be the best in the world. But this isn't the case. In reality, you just need to be the best in your world.

In other words, you need to be seen as an authority by your ideal audience, and make sure you're accessible by hanging out where they do.

And the people who really are world authorities on a subject? Well, they're your coaches and mentors. They're the people you learn from.

## MAKE COMPLICATED, EASY

Accounting, like any profession, is full of jargon, acronyms and complicated formulas. You can lead by making this information accessible to non-accountants.

You can take something hard and make it easy.

You can, for example, turn boring articles into audios and videos and complicated tables into metaphors. You can take all you've learned from your exams and turn it into insights and examples that use well-known figures and companies.

Comparing Jean-Christophe Novelli to Keith Floyd offers a great example. Before I founded TwentyTwo Agency and The Pioneering Practice Programme, I worked as an event director, which included running The Restaurant Show in London.

At the time, Jean-Christophe Novelli was the celebrity chef. I loved his TV programmes and his cooking demonstrations but, most of all, I loved his restaurant. In fact, because I enjoyed his food so much, I decided to buy one of his cookery books: "Your Place or Mine?".

The blurb described it as "Cooking at home with restaurant style". But could I make a single one of the recipes?

No.

They were simply too complicated. He might have been a leader and an authority on French cuisine, but his food just wasn't accessible.

Now compare him to Keith Floyd, another of the earliest celebrity chefs. His programmes are still shown online today, sharing his travels around the world and his cooking – all while he was drinking wine as fast as the French could make it.

Interestingly, though, I never bought one of his cookery books. Why?

Because it was enough to watch his demonstration, realise he'd used a maximum of five or so ingredients (of which butter and wine were two) and then have a go myself.

Keith Floyd inspired us by making the complicated easy. He showed us ways to enjoy dishes from around the world in the comfort of our own home.

Jean-Christophe Novelli's recipes, however, were so complicated that even with step-by-step instructions they were impossible to follow.

That's why you need to be like Keith Floyd. You need to make things easy, fun and entertaining for your audience.

## THE MORE YOU TEACH, THE MORE YOU LEARN

One of the current buzz phrases around the accounting profession is "trusted adviser". Yet, when it comes to stepping into the role, people are often hesitant. If this sounds like you, then remember: There's no better way to become a master of something than to teach it.

You can start by teaching the basics to beginners, i.e. to those who know nothing at all about the subject. That way, you can't help but be an authority! And it doesn't matter how many people have done it before you – or are doing it at the same time as you, if you do it well and inject your personality, businesses and students will flock to learn from you.

Gradually, as you teach, you'll start to develop and be able to share your own insights and understanding of topics. And, as you add depth to your own learning, you'll be able to pass this on through more in-depth and richer content.

Before you know it, you'll be the authority that we spoke of.

## IT'S NOT ABOUT YOU

You're not setting out to become an authority to satisfy your ego. You're doing it to help your readers and clients. Every time you fear to share an insight online, it's your ego kicking in by making it about you.

Know-it-alls have a tough time because they're constantly blowing their own trumpet. When you try to position yourself as the smartest guy in the room people don't like it.

On the other hand, when you approach your subject with expertise, modesty and a sincere desire to help, you'll find fans and evangelists who'll have your back when someone wants to take a pop at you.

By starting from the desire to help, you'll build trust and soon be seen as a leading authority.

## HOW TO CONVEY CREDIBILITY AND STATUS

Being seen as an authority will gain you the trust and confidence of your audience. That's why it's so important if you want your firm to be successful.

It'll bring you opportunities including:

- **Credibility & Trust:** Prospects will feel confident about choosing your firm.

- **Visibility:** You'll be able to spread your message further and be the first person people think of when they need help.
- **Client Acquisition:** You'll gain more clients and earn higher fees (as you'll have the edge when prospects are choosing a firm to work with).
- **Easier Sales Conversions:** Instead of having to sell yourself, people will approach you because of your expertise. In a knock-on effect, your practice will grow faster because sales are easier.
- **More Value:** As you become more visible, you'll reach more of your target market, which will push the value of your services up.
- **Easier Expansion:** The transition to expanding your firm into new markets will be smoother.
- **Increased Confidence:** Realising you know more about your chosen field than many or most firms will increase your confidence. Confidence instils confidence and prospects will be attracted to your practice.

## NEVER FAKE IT UNTIL YOU MAKE IT

Before you can establish yourself as an authority you need to become one. To do so, you need to learn everything possible about your chosen subject.

This is what one of our clients, Karl, did when he saw there was a gap in the market to help people with inheritance tax planning.

Even better, not only was there a gap in the market, but it was an area that he loved, too.

Karl gave up his evenings and weekends to study and pass a series of exams. Today, he's sharing his expertise and is well on the way to becoming a recognised authority on the topic.

Maybe you're already an authority on something? If so, then make sure you're sharing your knowledge with your audience by leveraging the Authority Practice Process™.

## THE AUTHORITY PRACTICE PROCESS™

Before you decide what you'd like to be an authority on, there are several points you need to bear in mind.

If your topic's too broad, you'll struggle to stand out and cut through the online hubbub. Alternatively, if you try to cover too many topics, you'll overwhelm yourself, confuse your prospects and be seen as a jack of all trades, master of none.

To illustrate, here's the example of an online coach I've followed for a few years. When they first started they were a relationship coach.

Next they moved on to confidence coaching, then business and finally, in their most recent incarnation, they became a bitcoin specialist.

The effect of this is that whereas their business once attracted opportunities and clients, it now attracts negative feedback and lacks credibility.

They're neither an authority nor a success.

That's why you must never fake it until you make it. And, once you've chosen your specialism, stick with it. I've been involved in marketing for 26 years, which is what enables me to be an authority.

How much would you trust me if I told you I was a marketing expert but most of my life I'd been an accountant?

## THE POWER OF A PROMISE

It doesn't matter how big or small, once I've promised my daughter Annabelle I'll do something I have to do it. Otherwise, hearing the words "But mummy, you promised" are enough to break my heart and, more importantly, to break her trust in me.

The same is true for clients. If you don't deliver on your promises, you'll destroy their trust.

You must be able to uphold the promises that you – as an authority – have committed to. So never, ever, think you can wing it.

EXERCISE

To help decide what you'd like to become an expert on, first think about where you are today:

- Is there anything I'm already an expert at?
- What promises can I make (and keep) that position me as an expert?
- What am I best known for?

Then think about where you'd like to be:

- What areas do I need to develop?
- What promises would I like to make in the future, but don't yet feel comfortable about?
- What's the one thing that I'd really like to be known for?

Finally, think about how you're going to get there:

- To develop myself in the right direction, I'll...?
- To feel comfortable making those promises, I'll...?
- To become an authority on this one thing, I need to...?

## THE ZERO MOMENT OF TRUTH

Whether we're shopping for cornflakes, concert tickets or a honeymoon in Paris, the internet has changed how we decide what to buy. Google calls the start of this decision-making process the "zero moment of truth", or ZMOT. ZMOT refers to the start of the buying process when the consumer researches a product prior to purchase.

What does this mean for your accounting practice?

Well, just like cornflakes, your practice has its own ZMOT. What your audience finds will determine how much they trust you, your firm and your services.

Before they get to this point, prospects will have placed you and your practice under the microscope to compare you to your competitors, follow your social media channels, check your online testimonials and judge your website.

When Google coined the term in 2011, they also determined that prior to buying a service or product, the average number of pieces of content consumed – whether blogs, videos or books – was just over 10. In addition, 70% of people consuming content watched video, of which 28% watched at least 30 minutes and 20% watched over 60 minutes.

These statistics are important. They mean that you need to have created at least 60 minutes of video that people can watch if they're to choose you over a competitor. But it doesn't stop there.

## THE 15/12 FORMULA

According to eMarketer, Google and Ipos Media people now spend an average of 15 hours researching a company before they buy from them. Prospects also look at an average of 12 pieces of content before they've built sufficient trust to reach out to you.

These are important numbers that it pays to keep in mind when you approach content creation.

These 12 pieces of content will be consumed in a number of different ways, they might be:

- Watched (videos or speaking engagements)
- Listened to (podcasts or radio interviews)
- Read (articles, blogposts, testimonials or social media posts)
- Interacted with (scorecards, tests or calculators)

That's why a pioneering practice must ensure they cover all these bases.

Recently, during a meeting with the two partners of an accounting practice, it was an absolute pleasure to listen to their banter – their personalities shone and one of them had an incredibly infectious laugh. I was quick to point out that they'd be great on video together. Whilst one was initially reticent, by the end of the meeting they were looking forward to creating some great video content for their website.

Similarly, whilst initially the idea might fill some of you with dread, I promise that once you're speaking on a subject you're passionate about, you won't even notice the camera's rolling.

Some of the conversations I have with partners in accounting practices can last for hours, yet they're so informative that I enjoy every minute.

So never underestimate your knowledge and expertise. Share value and become more vital.

## BUILDING AN AUTHORITY PLAN™

Now you've decided what you want to be an authority on, it's time to establish a plan to raise your visibility, engage and connect with your audience and convert them into clients.

Your authority plan should include:

- Where you can share free content (videos and articles etc.) that positions you as an expert.

- The kind of website you need to showcase your authority (that presents you solving your client's hot buttons).
- The content (whitepapers and eBooks etc) you can create in exchange for prospects sharing their email address with you.
- Where you can speak to showcase your expertise,
- The presentations you can create and deliver via webinars.
- The events your firm can run to position you locally.
- Any awards you can apply for to increase your credibility.
- Any case studies you can create to showcase your expertise.

We all know it's tough to grow an accounting practice today. There's more competition than ever and the days when clients based their buying decision on price alone are long gone. They want more and they're prepared to pay for it.

By positioning yourself as an authority, however, you'll no longer feel frustrated. Accounting software will support your practice rather than compete with it. As the authority, people will choose you over cheaper accountants.

Ultimately, you'll feel more fulfilled.

Fiona Hotston Moore, from Ensors Chartered Accountants, is a great example of an authority.

Fiona's a chartered accountant and tax adviser with a distinguished career history in forensic accountancy. She's a practising member of the Academy of Experts, an associate member of Resolution, on the panel of the ICAEW President's Appointment scheme, an Accredited Counter Fraud Specialist, and has enabled Ensors to join the Network of Independent Forensic Accountants (NIFA).

In national recognition of her contribution to the industry, in 2017 she also won Partner of the Year award at the British Accountancy Awards.

Fiona combines a hands-on, proactive approach with extensive specialist knowledge and commercial experience. As a keen commentator, she also writes regularly for the Ensors blog and Huffington Post.

If I ever need an accountant who specialises in forensic accountancy, Fiona would be my accountant of choice.

Who are you the accountant of choice for?

If you can't answer that yet, your goal over the next year is to follow the steps I've outlined above so that you can.

# STRATEGY 6 - AUTOMATION

You've probably heard about marketing automation. You may even know what it is. But the chances are you haven't deployed a solution yet, and neither are you clear on how it fits within your accounting practice.

Marketing automation seems to be the only solution to the major changes brought to us by technology. For an accounting practice to be successful they need to embrace digital marketing and communication services.

To compete in today's marketplace, accounting practices need to maintain an excellent relationship with existing clients and be able to anticipate their future needs. Using marketing automating tools gives firms more insights into their prospects' interests, behaviour and buying intentions.

If you still need convincing, here are some compelling statistics concerning users of marketing automation:

- 80% saw their number of leads increase and 77% their number of conversions increase. (VR Insight)
- 10% saw an increase in sales pipeline contribution. (Forrester Research)
- 20% increased their sales opportunities from nurtured leads versus non-nurtured leads after deploying a lead-nurturing program. (DemandGen)

However, whilst the above figures should have convinced you, choosing and implementing the right tools to automate your marketing isn't an easy decision. As with all technology, a marketing automation system is only as good as the effort you put into it – despite the word "automation", you still need to set it up and keep it working smoothly.

A marketing automation system often uses a platform that enables you to execute marketing campaigns across a number of platforms such as email, social media and your website. You also have the ability to personalise and automate the repetitive tasks associated with follow-up.

Marketing automation enables you to engage and nurture your leads and prospects. It's a little like taking care of a plant:

- Leads generated by your marketing campaign are the seeds.
- Your email follow-ups water and fertilise the seeds to make sure they grow.
- Sales are the fruit you harvest at the end of the process.

## THE THREE PILLARS

To explain where automation fits within your marketing, every plan or campaign you run involves three pillars:

- Strategy
- Tactics
- Tools.

However, although every marketing plan or campaign has to be designed in that order, more often than not at least one pillar gets forgotten or ignored.

Some people, for example, start by spending days overthinking tools. Rather than starting with strategy: "Who's my target market? What are their pains and how can I reach them?", they fret about whether to use MailChimp or ActiveCampaign to send out their newsletter, or whether they should use social media, referral marketing or SEO to generate leads.

To show you why they're so important, I'll explain each pillar in more detail.

## PILLAR 1: STRATEGY

There are four ingredients to consider when putting together a successful marketing strategy. You need to think about each one carefully, and revisit them as your firm grows and changes. Much of this work will have been done when you created your accounting practice, but let's revisit it quickly below:

1. **Specialisation**: Remember, you can't be all things to all people. Too many practices make the mistake of offering too many services, to too many types of clients, at too many prices,

in too many ways. As I've explained, this isn't the road to growth.

2. **Differentiation:** Success depends on your being better than your competitors in a clear way. The key to differentiation lies in understanding your competitors, knowing who they are and what makes them special. Then you need to understand why your ideal client's buying from them, and how you can change this. This is your USP (Unique Selling Proposition).

3. **Segmentation (niche):** If you decide to segment (niche) your market (for example by specialising in helping lawyers, property investors or start-ups) you'll need to divide potential clients into separate market segments. You'll need to understand and have a dedicated plan for each, plus identify the key characteristics and problems of each potential ideal client.

4. **Focus:** Once you've applied specialisation, differentiation and segmentation, you need to focus your resources – time, money and energy – on an outcome. Start with the end in mind. What's your desired outcome? Is it to generate more clients? To increase referrals? Or to grow profit by 30% over the next 24 months?

Once you know what you're focusing on, you can work out your strategy. Remember to allow at least a year to refine it. Only testing, measuring and tweaking in response to successes and failures will allow you to optimise your strategy and obtain the results you were hoping for.

Once your strategy's in place, it's time to move on to Pillar 2: Tactics.

## PILLAR 2: TACTICS

To reach your goal you need to have specific actions – tactics – in place.

Tactics are the highly practical things you need to do in your accounting practice - every day, week or month - to reach your desired outcome. Having a strong foundation (strategy) in place will ensure the tactics you use yield results.

Tactics include social media marketing, SEO (search engine optimisation), speaking, networking, events and email campaigns.

## THE MONEY MAP™

The Money Map – specific tactics to take someone from not knowing or trusting your accounting practice to signing up to work with you – is something I teach in our training programmes and workshops.

A Money Map must include at least three sections:

- a channel to get your information out there
- a client magnet (a way to obtain contact details)
- a conversion tool (event, webinar or meeting)

So it might look something like this:

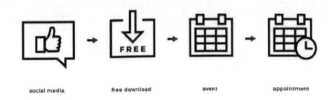

A prospect spots you on social media and downloads your eBook. Next they book to come to one of your events, where they set up another appointment with you at which they sign up to your services.

Or this:

After sending a direct mail letter to a prospect, you follow up with a phone call to invite them to an event, at which they decide to buy your services.

## PILLAR 3: TOOLS

The last pillar is to identify the tools you need to implement and leverage each tactic. Automation sits within this pillar. However, because there are so many tools available, many accounting practices become overwhelmed and unable to make a decision.

Some even end up investing heavily in tools they don't actually need to pay for – there are many low-cost or even free alternatives out there. For example:

- Excel and Google Analytics (both free) may be all you need to monitor your monthly marketing reporting – sophisticated platforms costing £700 a month simply aren't necessary for most small and medium-sized practices.

- A monthly newsletter can be created and sent out using Mailchimp for free rather than spending £2000 setting up a CRM programme with additional hefty monthly costs. Unless you're planning a complicated marketing campaign with "tags" and "rules" this is a complete waste of money.

- On the other hand, you could spend hours running your social media platforms manually when £6 per month would give you access to scheduling tools.

- Similarly, you can either spend a small fortune on microphones, lights and a camera to create videos – or simply use your iPhone for free.

- Great tools for webinars include WebinarJam, GoToWebinar and Zoom.

## WHAT CAN WE LEARN FROM THE ROMANS?

I'm a huge fan of the Monty Python film "Life Of Brian". In one of my favourite scenes, three characters are bickering. It goes something like this:

*Reg:* And what have the Romans ever given us in return?
*Xerxes:* The aqueduct.
*Reg:* Oh yeah, yeah they gave us that. Yeah. That's true.
*Masked Activist:* And the sanitation!
*Matthias:* And the roads...
*Another Masked Activist:* Irrigation...
*Other Masked Voices:* Medicine... Education... Health...
*Reg:* All right... all right... but apart from better sanitation and medicine and education and irrigation and public health and roads and a freshwater system and baths and public order... what have the Romans done for us?

You see the Romans built stuff. They built aqueducts and roads and made sure that they had systems in place so that everything could run quickly and smoothly. We can learn a lot from their example.

Without systems to make your life easier, you have to do the same thing over and over again. Imagine what life was like before the Romans built aqueducts. Imagine how much time and effort was spent collecting just a couple of buckets of water each day. Then multiply this by 365.

This is what it's like for many accounting practices. Each new client is generated by one referral and needs lengthy sales meetings – sometimes more than one – to clinch. No wonder practices eventually run out of time and energy. They're exhausted!

Instead of running your practice like this, build an automated system and leverage tools. That way, instead of a trickle, you'll attract a flood of new clients.

## THINKING AHEAD

I drive my husband mad. Often it's because of the speed at which I think – I'm nearly always one step ahead of him with my actions and thoughts.

I put much of this down to the fact that I've spent years thinking one step ahead in my business so that I can automate as much as possible.

By thinking one step ahead, you'll be able to provide a better experience for your clients and audience. Whether they're reading your articles, watching your videos or downloading your free eBooks, automation will help you achieve this smoothly and at scale.

To recap, let me share some examples of how the three pillars work:

### Strategy

- Specialisation: Outsourced accounting
- Differentiation: Tech-savvy
- Segmentation: Tech start-ups
- Focus (outcome): 20 new clients in 12 months, each paying a minimum £2k per year

### Tactics

1. eBook to gain email subscribers that can be downloaded from your website and delivered straight to their inboxes.
   **Automation tools:** Wordpress website, MailChimp.
2. Autoresponders – six emails are sent after a subscriber has downloaded the eBook.
   **Automation tool: MailChimp.**
3. 10 social media updates across different platforms every day for 30 days to increase visibility.
   **Automation tools:** Facebook, Twitter, LinkedIn or Buffer (scheduled in one go).

This is how to leverage your time and effort using automation tools.

Create a strong strategy, choose the right tactics to fulfil it, then use automation tools to leverage your time and effort.

No one has time to carry out marketing manually. Automation will build freedom into your accounting practice and allow you to deliver over and over again.

By investing a little time upfront, you can create great marketing strategies that ensure you're more visible, vital and valued.

# Part 3
# SALES CONVERSIONS

In order to persuade a prospect to buy, you need to create the right buying environment. Environment dictates the performance of your marketing and the success of your sales.

Think about your current environment for converting prospects into clients. Do you speak to them over the phone or invite them to lengthy meetings?

Every client has two barriers to overcome in deciding to buy:

1. How long will it take?
2. How much pressure will be placed on them?

To deal with the first, how often do you ask a prospect, "How much time have you put aside to speak/meet today?" The key to success lies in knowing the answer to this.

And it works both ways. Equally, you don't want one prospect taking up your whole day when you have other people to see. Giving the impression that you have all the time in the world will mean they fail either consciously or subconsciously to respect you.

You need to create an environment that makes clear to prospects that you're in demand.

Scarcity's a powerful influencer. Ensuring that a prospect sees you have a queue of people who want to do business with you will create the right impression.

Now, to deal with the second barrier, do you remember the old saying: "People love to buy stuff, but they hate being sold to."

Why do they hate it? Because no one wants to be put under pressure – particularly not when they're considering a purchase. Pressure will never create a conducive sales environment. Consumers are savvy and no longer respond to the sales patter that door-to-door insurance salesmen once thrived on.

In this part of the book, we'll be taking a look at creating a buying environment that leverages your time, your prospects' time, and alleviates the need for a pressurised sale.

# STRATEGY 7 - EVENTS

To start, I'd like to share how I met my first-ever pioneering practice. I'd just launched my own business and had no idea how to make myself known locally. My experience was based on running exhibitions all over the world, while my specific marketing experience covered brochures and corporate campaigns – but all with access to a substantial budget. Running my own small business was proving to be a different ball game altogether.

I decided to search out networking events and it was at this point that I came across The Wow Company.

The Wow Company was running an event at my local Holiday Inn, with 70 attendees and, as guest speaker, an inspiring entrepreneur called Lara Morgan. It was the first time I'd heard of either her or the company, but first impressions were good. Peter Czapp, Wow's co-founder, introduced Lara and the event went well. I met some people I'm still in touch with today, and then I went home.

Two months later I attended another event, at Winchester Science Centre, where the guest speaker (again introduced by Peter) was Spencer Gallagher.

Fast-forward two months and you'd have found me at another of their events, this time at the amazing Rose Bowl in Southampton.

Although, as usual, Peter introduced the guest speaker, I also spent quite a bit of time speaking with Paul Bulpitt, another of the company's co-founders.

Less than a month later I signed up to be their client. Why? Because I'd come to trust the practice. Even more importantly, because I'd started to build a relationship with Paul and Peter the on-boarding process was smooth and straightforward.

Rather than having to travel to their offices for a lengthy meeting, I signed up with Paul over the phone in a process that took minutes.

I was assigned a key accounts manager and since then all our meetings have been held via Skype. Other communication has been mostly via phone and email.

So why did I choose The Wow Company as my accountants? As the section heading suggests: events.

## THE POWER OF RUNNING LIVE EVENTS

Imagine a platform which allows you to share your knowledge, build relationships, offer advice, answer questions and position yourself as an authority.

Furthermore, this platform enables you to on-board many new clients in one go, thereby saving you time and leveraging your efforts.

Accounting practices need to seize every opportunity to build relationships, generate goodwill and earn the trust of audiences and prospective clients. Equally, audiences need more than just a pitch when evaluating solutions or making purchasing decisions.

Events offer a unique opportunity for prospects to interact with your practice and to gain a first-hand sense of your focus, perspective, values and personality. Mastering event marketing is an essential tactic in building your bottom line.

To make an impact, events must be memorable. Just like those of the Wow Company – who've progressed from local events around the Salisbury area to quarterly ones in the centre of London. Each of their events now attracts hundreds of attendees, creating an outstanding experience for existing and prospective clients alike.

Of course, most accounting practices want events to be more than just a staged advertisement for their brand.

A well-run event creates a lasting and powerful impression of all that your accounting practice can deliver. But, by allowing people to experience and interact with you, your team and your service, you're also forming the basis for strong relationships and trust.

## WHY DO PEOPLE GO TO BUSINESS EVENTS?

The answer lies with our basic human needs, described in psychologist Abraham Maslow's "Hierarchy of Needs" as:

1. **Biological and Physiological:** air, food, drink, shelter, warmth, sex, sleep.
2. **Safety:** protection from the elements, security, order, law, stability, freedom from fear.
3. **Love** and Belonging: friendship, intimacy, trust and acceptance, receiving and giving affection and love. Affiliating, being part of a group (family, friends, work).
4. **Esteem:** which Maslow broke down into two categories: (i) esteem for oneself (dignity, achievement, mastery, independence) and; (ii) the desire for reputation or respect from others (status, prestige).
5. **Self-Actualisation:** realising personal potential, self-fulfilment, seeking personal growth and peak experiences. A desire "to become everything one is capable of becoming".

No other marketing and sales channel enables you to fulfil the hierarchy of needs quite like running an event. This is even more true when you're able to build a community through running a series of events. Next, I'll run through some of those needs again to explain why.

**Safety:** Going to an event feels safe for most people. They don't have to overcome a psychological barrier to attend. Unlike in a 1:1 meeting, prospects can check you out without feeling they have to buy. Plus lots of other people are going so it must be the right decision.

**Belonging:** Going to an event means you're part of something bigger than yourself, that you're part of a community. Most people there are probably looking for the same or similar answers to you. An event provides social proof that you're making the right decision by being there. You're not alone.

**Esteem:** Going to an event makes us feel we're working towards the independence – as Maslow pointed out – we want; that we're taking action to achieve our esteem needs. Do you remember how chuffed you felt after the last event that allowed you to share information about your business? A good event will allow your audience to have great conversations and leave one step nearer to independence.

**Self-Actualisation:** By going to an event you're seeking to improve your knowledge and better yourself. Whether it's two hours or three days, the time you've invested symbolises that you're investing in your personal development to realise your potential.

**Biological and Physical:** Going to an event can even fulfil your most basic needs. You're inside, warm, and often accompanied by food and a drink!

In short, events make people feel good.

Now that you understand why events are so powerful, let's explore what kind you can run.

## RUNNING A MASTERMIND GROUP

For two years I belonged to a Mastermind Group held at The Ritz in London. At each monthly event I was surrounded by a likeminded community. I learnt new things. I worked on mastery of my skills. I worked towards independence. And it all took place in an amazing environment with great food and water on tap.

This peer-to-peer mentoring group of 20 people cost less than £100 per month and ticked off every stage in Maslow's hierarchy of needs. I felt great!

With very little effort you could set up your own Mastermind Group. You just need to make sure that it's mutually beneficial to all members and offers a combination of brainstorming, education, peer accountability and support.

Mastermind events, sometimes called inner circles, are usually monthly and can be either half or full days. The investment starts at around £100 per month but can go up to £500 or more.

Persuading 10 people to sign up could add an additional £60,000 per year to your bottom-line. You could offer the service to your best clients, or set up a group for prospects who aren't yet clients.

If you decide on the latter, after a year you may have been able to build relationships with attendees to the extent that they migrate their accounting needs to your firm. If so, within 12 months you could add £100,000 to your bottom line – not bad for six days work a year.

Not only that, but your group has such a great reputation that there's a queue of people wanting to join, so you have to open another group.

Today, accountants are often told they should be a "trusted adviser" to clients. Running a Mastermind Group will enable you to be seen as an adviser whilst leveraging the knowledge in the room. By facilitating the event, you provide the attendees a platform from which to help one another.

Of course, running an event where people commit to even £100 per month needs financial commitment and a sales conversation to persuade people to join. However, other events exist which offer a lower barrier to entry and which your practice can use to build relationships with attendees and sell them your services.

So let's explore a few.

## NETWORKING EVENTS

Networking is a supportive system that allows individuals and groups with a common interest to share information and services. Most often networking events take place to facilitate business activity. Business people and entrepreneurs meet to form business relationships and to recognise, create, or act upon business opportunities, to share information and seek potential partners for ventures.

Organising networking events positions you as an enabler of relationships and a linchpin of the community. You'll be seen as the go-to accounting practice and will be at the front of people's minds the next time they need help or advice. Exactly as the Wow Company did with their events.

Networking events can take place at any time during the day or evening. However, if you want to attract a certain kind of client then remember to consider the time that will best suit them. The attendees' schedule, not yours, is key.

## FULL- OR MULTI-DAY EDUCATIONAL EVENTS

For some accounting practices, the essential goal of an event is to educate their audience.

If you're at the vanguard of a brand-new technology or industry (such as cloud accounting a few years ago, or Making Tax Digital now), you'll need to educate an entire market about the possibilities of your solutions. If so, a half- or full-day event will enable you to educate your attendees whilst simultaneously positioning you as an authority.

And don't forget you need to provide 15 hours of content for your audience to trust you. An all-day event will tick off eight of these immediately. (Although the content and methodology outlined below will be the same for a seminar or webinar.)

Events are also a brilliant way to improve your retention rates – whether of staff, clients, partners or suppliers. They allow you to recognise and thank key people, extending a personal touch and enhancing your relationships.

Creating a unique experience – the sky (or your budget) is literally the limit – will leave your guests in no doubt that yours is the accounting practice for them.

Every company I've worked with has had a massive return on their investment through the opportunities, credibility, reputation, relationships and clients events lead to.

However, some I've attended have been lacklustre, disappointing and left people wanting more.

You can't expect to have a successful event without a few specific activities in place.

## SHOW ME THE MONEY

If you've ever been to London's Covent Garden you'll have seen some excellent street performers, including jugglers, musicians and singers.

But, at the end of their performance, what did you do? Did you clap? Smile? Comment to your family or friends on their performance?

Most likely, you simply moved on to the next thing that caught your eye. When what the performers really wanted was for you to put some money in their hat.

It's the same with events. Companies run an event, an audience attends, learns, claps, comments to their friends how great it was, and then leaves.

In other words, they don't put money in the hat.

Running a "nice" – rather than a conversion – event is a major problem.

That's why a crucial section of our Pioneering Practice Programme is on how to run a conversion event. I'll introduce the key principles now.

## CONVERSION EVENTS

A conversion event allows you to deliver great content, educate your audience and help them understand their problem – all while positioning yourself as the solution to it.

By following the Traffic Light Method™ you build their desire to work with you and, at the end, when you invite them to sign up, they do.

However, as well as the Traffic Light Method, you also need some other specific elements.

## SIMON SAYS: "OWN THE ROOM"

From the moment a potential client steps into the room a game starts to play out. And, although what I'm about to share with you was not something (as an introvert) I ever thought I'd be able to do, after a few tries I saw what an impact it had on an event's success.

If you've ever been to one of my events you'll already have experienced it. If not, this alone is worth the day out of the office. As if you can get your head around it you'll be well on your way to smashing your own conversion event.

The idea, which I learnt from my business coach, Taki, comes from the game Simon Says. As in "Simon says 'Put your hands on your head'". And, when we hear the person at the front of the room say this, what do we do? We put our hands on our head.

Simon's in control. That's how Simon Says works. People love to do what they're asked.

So I use the Simon Says method the moment I step on stage. This is how it plays out – every time.

Me: "Raise Your Right hand."
Audience: raises their right hand.
Me: "Now wave it around a bit."
Audience: waves their hand around a bit.
Me: "OK, put your hand on the shoulder of the person next to you, give them a shake and say, 'Oh no! She's interactive!'"

Two important things take place during this process:

1. **I break the audience's mood.** Maybe their train journey was delayed or they hit a traffic jam. Maybe they had an argument with their spouse or their kids were late for school. That's why it's so important to break their mood – it might not have been the most receptive.

2. **The audience did as I asked – five times.** And it always works. I instruct, the audience responds.

In other words, I owned the room.

During the first few minutes of any event you need to accomplish three things, to:

- grab your audience's attention
- create a connection
- obtain their permission

If you'd like to experience one of my Pioneering Practice full-day events first-hand, then you can check out the dates and sign up on my website **www.twentytwo.agency**. (I'll even let you into a little secret... that's the end of the interactive activities!)

## SHOW YOUR EXPERTISE

Having worked with many, many accounting practices, I know that people usually love the teaching/education part of events, but hate asking for sales at the end of it.

It's why accounting practices struggle with a return on investment: education and sales are seen as separate things.

However, as long as you alternate between amber content (solutions to their problems) and green content (case studies) to back up each of your points, then your audience will automatically see you as the solution and want to sign up for your services.

Once you've mapped out your core content, you also need to consider any objections your audience might have – from not really understanding how cloud accounting works, to simply not wanting the upheaval of moving accountants – that could stop them from working with your practice.

Finally, you need to highlight the specific areas your accounting services cover – whether cloud accounting, access to a specific App, quarterly meetings or Mastermind Groups – and showcase what working with you and your practice will be like.

Once you've done all the prep work you'll have a seamless presentation that positions you as an authority, educates the audience, illuminates their problems, overcomes their objections, showcases how your services will help and outlines the experience of working with you.

In other words, the event becomes a mixture of teaching and selling. You're teaching them what they want to know and what they want.

## MAKE THE SALE

A common misconception is that technology's making accounting services obsolete – that a businesses can install Xero accounting software and do everything themselves.

To overcome this thinking, your event needs to make the ramifications of companies going it alone and keeping their accounting in-house clear.

The best way to do this is by creating some tension. For example, challenge them whether they'd like to hear your offer or not by saying: "If you want to hear about our XYZ service I'd be really happy to have a casual conversation – but it's also totally cool if you don't!"

You can then share your services (and how working with your practice will pan out for them over the next few years) with those who ask. In fact, it's not unusual to sign up 30-40% of the room using this method once you've mastered it.

Never try to make a sale to everyone in the room. By offering an "out", some people will choose to stay in.

Accountants can rock events. You just need the know-how.

# STRATEGY 8 - CAMPAIGNS

Recently, while I was being interviewed on the radio, the interviewer – a partner from Champ Consultants, an accounting practice in Surrey – asked me about the nine key strategies I discuss in this book.

Specifically, she asked whether it mattered in which order they're implemented. She wanted to know whether, for example, you can dive in and start running events before you've educated your market, or built yourself up as an authority.

My answer was simple: No.

Apart from the ninth strategy – experience, which you need to implement within the previous eight – to be successful you need to follow the rest in order.

However excited you might be at the thought of running an event, unless you go into it with a clear idea of your ideal client, a strong brand in the marketplace, knowledge of where your ideal clients hang out and how to make sure you're visible to them there, you'll fail.

This chapter brings the previous seven together, and shows you the real power of running a pioneering campaign.

## SELLING ONE AT A TIME

In my late teens and early twenties I worked as a sales rep, booking exhibition stands for big industry events and selling advertising space in magazines. I sold to prospects one at a time and was excited every time I received an enquiry. In fact, if I made a few sales a month I was satisfied. It was a slog, and underwhelming.

When I first launched my business in 2009 I approached sales in exactly the same way. I tried to win clients one at a time. I was excited by each enquiry. If I made a couple of sales a month I was satisfied. Yes – it was a slog, and underwhelming.

Then I realised the power of running my business in an organised and active manner to achieve a specific goal. Of building a marketing machine, rather than just doing marketing. This machine enables me to fill online and offline events at which I can educate 10 to 100 people at a time.

Now these events are mapped out 12 months in advance and my marketing has one focus: to fill them and build good relationships with the people who attend.

At the time of writing my calendar has three in-person events a year and, in addition, every three weeks I run a webinar. Having this mapped out 12 months in advance means I know what my focus is every day, week and month.

Another thing I realised was that running my marketing in 90-day cycles, each with a particular focus, would allow me to complete more in those 90 days than most people achieve in a year. This focus enables me to leverage my time and achieve things others only dream of.

Writing this book, for example, has been accomplished in a 90-day window. I locked myself away for a week at the end of January to write my first draft, then didn't revisit it until the end of February. It's now the middle of March, the final edit will have been completed by the end of the month, and the book will be ready by the end of April. (I have to finish it by then because in May I start my next 90-day cycle.)

I allow 90 days of focused and organised activity for each specific goal.

It's taken me a long time to get into the flow of running my business in this way, but it's been transformational. I remember my business coach, Taki, teaching me that cash flow follows my calendar. In other words, my calendar dictates the success of my business.

Does your calendar reflect where you're at in yours? If you want to grow your business, for example, how much time have you scheduled for this?

## CAMPAIGN METHOD

As an accountant (or marketing expert within an accounting practice) you'll understand the need for a process-driven plan. One which maps out the marketing activities that need doing and – most importantly – when.

Implementing a campaign requires that you carry out the necessary work at each stage in the method. If you skip a section, you'll miss opportunities.

## UNDERSTANDING THE PROCESS

Once you have a clear understanding of which market will value your services and who you want to work with, it's time to map out and execute your campaigns.

Campaigns require one thing above all else: focus.

Too many campaigns fail because firms choose to run three or four campaigns at once.

Whether it's to fill an event, launch a new service or generate more inbound leads, campaigns rarely work if you run more than one at a time. That's because your marketing message and your calls to action need to be consistent.

Two or more different messages will confuse your audience and stop them acting, i.e. signing up to your services. This is why focus is key.

Campaigns should combine various tools and tactics to drive prospects towards one specific action.

The best campaigns for an accounting firm are those that follow the Money Map. Focus on the tactics you need to fill an event and to persuade its attendees to buy your services.

## THE FOUR STEPS OF EVENT-MARKETING CAMPAIGNS

### Stage One: Hands-Up

After you've decided what kind of campaign you're going to run, and its objective, it's time to map your campaign.

When I first started running events, I hit on the method behind my success almost by accident. I was busy planning my first event in the City – an evening one, for a maximum of 15 people – but I was nervous. I was outside my comfort zone. I hadn't run an event for this particular audience before and the niche, the location and my positioning in the market place were all new to me. I wasn't yet a well-known authority, and the audience wouldn't have heard of me.

Still, I went ahead. I fixed a date, designed a few images for social media, and asked some friends to share details of the event and tell anyone who was interested to message me for more information.

Next thing I knew, one of my Facebook posts had over 20 people saying they were interested and a few others had tagged their friends. (At this point I hadn't even designed a sign-up form!)

You can imagine how chuffed I was, but the fantastic response led to a new problem: there were more people interested than the room could hold. I acted swiftly.

I used Eventbrite to put a sign-up form together and sent it to everyone who'd expressed interest, making sure I let them know that there were already over 20 people interested but we only had space for 15. Within hours the event was fully booked.

Although I didn't realise it at the time, I was already using the first part of the Traffic Light Method. I was disrupting people. I called the event Corporate Escape and by highlighting their pain I'd got their attention. A public show of hands meant that others felt comfortable sharing that they wanted to come, too. In fact, in a snowball effect, the more popular the event looked the less people wanted to miss out.
I now call this first stage of the campaign method, the Hands-Up stage. It uses the AIDA – Attention, Interest, Desire, Action – principle I learnt over 20 years ago when I worked for Marie Claire magazine. In other words, by knowing who my ideal client was, I was able to get their attention, persuade them to express interest and then build their desire by showing how popular the event was.

Apple uses the AIDA principle, too. Each time they announce the launch of their latest product well in advance to grab people's Attention. Then they get everyone to show Interest and talk about it by sharing its new gizmos. In this way they build Desire and persuade you to take Action by buying the product. Showing that demand is ten times bigger than supply builds excitement even further with the result that each launch day is met with long queues.

It's this visibility that I created through people "putting their hands up" on Facebook, or that Apple creates through the long queues outside its showrooms is what enables social proof to do the selling for you.

However, running an event isn't just about attracting an audience. It's also about attracting other opportunities.

### Stage Two: Sign-Up

Once people have put their hands up to express interest, you need to persuade them to commit by signing up. This is where the Traffic Light Method™ comes back into play.

During the Hands-Up stage you generated an audience who'd expressed an interest in hearing more about your event. Now you need to turn that interest into a commitment to attend.

During the sign-up stage you need to create both amber and green content by educating your audience on their pain/problem, and then positioning your firm as an authority and your event as the solution. This means that your content shouldn't only be educational, it also needs to include proof in the form of testimonials and case studies from past attendees or current clients.

Robert Frith, Director of Frith & Co Accountants, successfully fills his events using the Traffic Light Method™ and the AIDA principle. Although he doesn't run a niche practice, one of his specialisms – and something he's known as an authority on – is property tax. Much of this is down to the quarterly events he runs on the subject for around 40 attendees each time a mixture of his clients, the general public and local business people.

Before he even advertises each event he asks his clients and network if they're interested in attending. Any that say yes are asked to invite their friends and colleagues, and his assistant registers them.

By the time he begins marketing the event is already almost fully booked, which massively increases its appeal and positions Robert as someone in demand.

### Stage Three: Show-Up

Sometimes life gets in the way. Unless you've convinced people who've registered that's it's of the utmost importance, it's possible that no one will even show up for your event – especially if it's free.

To avoid this you need to stay in touch, highlighting (and reminding them of) the importance of attending through the use of education-based marketing and by building their excitement.

This regular contact is essential. People forget they've signed up to events. If they haven't had to invest any money, something as simple as a bad journey or being "a little tired" can be enough to have them heading straight home, or hitting the snooze button instead of getting up.

The Show-Up stage of your campaign marketing is most effective if you use a number of different tactics. These might include email, SMS or simply picking up the telephone. I'd also suggest that you continue to build great relationships with your registrants by connecting with them on social media.

If they're going to show up, you need to win their emotional investment and commitment.

### Stage Four: Pay-Up

Your campaign, however, doesn't stop once they've shown up. You've chosen to run the event to convert prospects into clients. That's why this stage is called Pay Up.

Whilst your ability to achieve this will depend on how much trust you can create at your event, you'll certainly maximise results by adding scarcity and qualification to the mix.

If 100 people attend, all of whom know you're only able to take on four clients this month, then it's likely more than four will want to pay up there and then. Conversely, knowing you have unlimited capacity won't create the urgency your audience needs to commit to working with you whilst they're in the room.

You also need to define who your service is for – and who it's not for. By highlighting your ideal client's traits, people can self-qualify and do your work for you. Prospects are more likely to pay up if their values, hot buttons and solutions align with those you've focused on.

To maximise conversions, be clear on who you can help and how.

## Stage Five: Follow-Up

Not everyone will buy from you there and then. Maybe they have a business partner who needs to agree first, or someone else holds the purse strings. Even if they award you 10 on the Trust Factor™, some prospects simply might not be able to buy immediately.

Whatever their reason for not signing up on the day, you can still convert them with effective follow-up.

That's why you need to nurture the relationships you've created with good quality content. You need to keep educating your audience, answering their questions, showing more social proof and overcoming any objections.

If you do everything you need to, when the time's right they'll buy.

Remember, for a prospect to feel they know, like and trust you and your firm enough to buy from you, they need to have spent 15 hours consuming your content. That's why they may come to more than one event, attend several webinars, follow your blog and watch your videos.

After 15 hours, those who are in the market to buy will do so.

## CAMPAIGN MARKETING FOR ACCOUNTANTS

Some accounting practices seem to believe that this approach to marketing is hard work and unnecessary. They're usually the same practices that struggle to bring in even half a million pounds per year in revenue. Having watched The Wow Company run campaigns for nearly 10 years, and other pioneering practices use event marketing and campaigns to fill their client lists, I can assure you that it's totally necessary.

Running events streamlines and focuses your marketing. As a bonus, each event will get easier to run and convert more prospects into clients. Your calendar will have set dates on which your practice can sell to a roomful of prospects and your marketing will gain rhythm and momentum.

EXERCISE

Decide on your 90-day campaign and event, then fix a date in your diary.

Map out the marketing content needed to maximise the effect of each stage:
- Hands-Up
- Sign-Up
- Show-Up
- Pay-Up
- Follow-Up

# STRATEGY 9 - EXPERIENCE

## WHAT DO MY CLIENTS WANT?

This is the question that every accounting practice should be asking itself, and the question that the savviest accounting practices already are.

Technology has handed the accounting profession unprecedented control over the ways in which your services are purchased, and the experience we can create for clients and prospects alike.

By leveraging technology well, we can create a strong advantage by being ever-present in consumers' lives.

More and more, we're expected to provide the level of service and satisfaction that consumers receive from Amazon, Uber and Apple, and customer experience is increasingly benchmarked by the speed and customer service of these firms.

Clients expect us to be "on" all the time. They expect emails to be returned instantly. They expect work to be completed faster and in a more streamlined way.

If they can get anything they want delivered to their home within 24 hours, why wouldn't they expect us to return an email as fast? Clients are now dictating the rules. They expect a "now" service, which means within five minutes of their making contact online.

Clients also expect to do business online. They assume we're on social media platforms and even insist on that social experience. They put as much trust in a Google review as they once did in a personal recommendation.

Pioneering accounting practices understand that it's no longer enough to compete on services. Research indicates that how an organisation delivers is just as important as what.

Accounting practices that make it easier for people to connect, will make inroads on their competition.

For real success, firms need to adapt processes, cultures and mind-sets to manage customer experience skilfully. This not only benefits our clients and our audience, but also our teams and our bottom lines.

Sadly, most accounting practices fail to deliver a compelling customer experience. If customer experience is on the agenda at all, it's often a disjointed effort that focuses on individual touchpoints rather than an overall system for delivering value. Focus needs to be on delivering value before, during, and after purchase.

According to McKinsey Digital Labs, customer behaviour and expectations are changing:

- 75% of online customers expect help within five minutes of making contact

- 61% of customers are more likely to buy from companies that deliver customer content
- 79% of consumers trust an online review as much as they do a personal recommendation

Our reputations used to be dictated by our firms, now it's dictated by our clients. Once upon a time what we said about our accounting practice was gospel. We could pick and choose which testimonials to share and if we were unfortunate enough to have delivered a bad service once or twice, the news rarely travelled far.

These days, however, if you fail to look after clients or don't treat your audience the way they expect, don't be surprised if their negative experience is shared with their online networks. In other words, with thousands of people across Facebook, Twitter, LinkedIn, and Google.

Furthermore, your desired audience now has the power of choice. They can choose the right accountant for them by doing their own research. They're no longer reliant on the buying information your firm provides – which means the information that they do see can't be manipulated.

If you do a bad job, clients will share this online and on social media platforms. And abdicating from using social media won't solve your problem. It simply means you won't even have the ability to monitor what's being said, or to get involved in the conversation.

Understanding this new way of recommending and referring should have a direct impact on how you run your accounting practice. A client wants more from your accounting firm, and if they don't get it they'll go to your competitors instead.

The good news is that technology allows you to provide more. The moment anyone searches online for an accountant, follows you on social media, comes to one of your events or becomes a client, you have the chance to "wow" them.

If you get it right, you'll be recommended and referred and have a community of fans. Get it wrong, however, and your name will be mud.

## LEARNING FROM PIONEERS IN OTHER INDUSTRIES

You can learn how to ingrain a "wow" experience in your own practice from pioneers in other industries:

**Apple:** Apple doesn't only sell computers or phones; it sells experiences. What makes someone choose an Apple product over a Microsoft one?

Simon Sinek, author of "Start With Why", suggests that Apple stands out from its competitors because it sells an attitude. As he points out, "Apple is just a computer company. There's nothing that distinguishes them structurally from any of their competitors."

Anyone can sell computers, but Apple focuses on the experience that comes with buying one of their products. To do this, they make sure their products are beautifully designed and user-friendly. In fact, they even employ a dedicated "box opener" to ensure that our experience on opening our new product is the one they want us to have. (And anyone who's ever purchased an Apple product knows how great an experience unboxing it is.)

But, to make sure we have that experience, the box opener needed to open an awful lot of boxes to get it right. So much work goes into creating the experience because it's the little things that leave a big impression.

**Amazon:** Amazon is a pioneer that continues to focus on delivering an exceptional customer experience. Although it isn't the only online retailer out there, the jaw-dropping fact is that its sales are now higher than the sales of the next 12 biggest retailers put together. That's because Amazon realises that in today's price-sensitive world it needs to create better customer experiences.

**Disney:** Disney World doesn't sell theme park tickets; it sells an experience. My own visit confirms this. My children have been to many theme parks, but not one of them left the memory that Disney World did. In fact, 4 years later, they still ask me daily when can we go back?

And it wasn't just the children that loved it. It was the holiday of a lifetime for all of us – all because of the experience that Disney created.

That's because Disney doesn't see itself as a theme park. Instead, everything it does is approached from the angle of being in the family entertainment business. And not only was Disney the pioneer in how to deliver this family entertainment experience, but no other theme park has been able to replicate it.

That's because when it comes to understanding its guests, Disney takes a "compass approach" to identifying and planning a list of customer experience touch points:

- North – needs
- West – wants
- South – stereotypes
- East – emotions.

**Needs:** When we talk about a client's needs, we're talking about the basics. If someone goes to a doctor, they might "need" medicine to get well. Similarly, if they come to you, they might "need" someone to do their taxes. Needs is about meeting their minimum requirements.

**Wants:** This is where you can kick clients' experience up a notch or two. If someone "wants" new strategies to help them save on taxes, for example, then providing this extra level of service allows you to start to differentiate yourself. You'll also give people more reason to return and to refer you.

**Stereotypes:** This is when you need to overcome any negative impressions clients might have of you or your business. A stereotypical view of an accountant might be that you're a necessary – but boring – commodity.

According to a recent poll in the magazine "Accountancy Age", 28% of respondents believed accountants lack a sense of humour, while only 4% perceived them to be fun. Although you and I know this isn't true, the fact that so many people believe it sets us a challenge. We need to be doing everything we can to promote that not only are we fun but also that, rather than a commodity, we play a key strategic development role and are central to the success of any business.

**Emotions:** We all know that emotions are more powerful than logic when it comes to making buying decisions. That's why it's so important to consider what makes our clients feel good about buying from us and then to focus on that when delivering our services.

To summarise then, here's what we can learn from Disney, Apple and Amazon:

- Strive to be different – don't settle for what your industry's already doing
- Don't focus on what you do, focus on why
- Make sure you include your customer experience strategy in your firm's vision
- Continue to innovate and to improve your customer experience

## EXCEL AND EXCEED

Whilst Apple, Disney and Amazon all offer great examples, it's also true that they have deep pockets and huge departments to work on creating the experiences they provide. But don't let this put you off creating your own remarkable experiences for clients. To illustrate how easy it can be, I'd like to share one of my own recent experiences.

## A STORY OF LOYALTY AND FIRST IMPRESSIONS

My hairdresser, Ollie, skipped town a few weeks ago. He'd been my hairdresser for over four years and when I found out he'd left the salon and moved away I was devastated. My loyalty wasn't with the salon but with him, however, and the moment I found out he'd gone I knew my time with them was over.

I decided to try "Elements", the salon across the road. It was more expensive but the interior was sumptuous and the receptionist was friendly so I booked an appointment for a hair colour. I had no idea what the experience would be like, I was just trying the salon "on" to see if it was a good fit.

A day before the appointment I received a questionnaire asking me what my biggest challenge with my hair was. I thought this was a nice touch. It meant I didn't need to go through the usual chit-chat when I met my new hairdresser. It also got me looking forward to my appointment.

When I arrived the next day, the receptionist took my coat and offered me a cup of tea. Nothing ground-breaking so far, but then things went up a notch.

After my initial consultation, I was told that as a new client I was entitled to a complimentary blow-drying session in the coming weeks, as well as a complimentary goodie bag filled with free samples.

I was hooked. During my colour, I'd already decided to commit to a cut the following day. The customer experience was so good that I knew I'd found my new hairdressers.

"Elements" had achieved what I call "Excel and Exceed".

**Excel at what you do. Exceed expectations.**

## THE FIRST 100 DAYS

This phrase typically refers to the first 100 days of the first term of a President of the United States of America. These first 100 days set the tone of their time in office. Their impact and rating during this time is measured – and you won't be surprised to hear that John F Kennedy had the highest ratings while Donald Trump has the lowest.

In exactly the same way, the first 100 days you work with a new client will set the tone of how they work with your accounting practice in the future.

The good news is that this on-boarding period doesn't have to be difficult. It can even be automated through a series of emails.

Imagine how new clients would feel if, when they sign up:

1.  They receive an email saying thank you and welcoming them to the team. (Using the word "team" will make them feel part of something.) The email also outlines the departments in your practice and the key people they might need to speak to depending on their query. (This is particularly useful because it stops partners being contacted unnecessarily and directs the right enquires to the right people.)

2. A day later they receive another email with a link to a customer-experience team member's online diary. (Or, if you're a small firm, to that of a partner or another member of your team.) This allows them to book a 30-minute call to go through what working with you will be like.

3. During this 30-minute call, your practice tells them about the secure systems they can use to share information with you, plus how often you'll speak to them and how they can best get in touch. You can also set out the rules of how they need to act – such as sharing their accounts information.

   You can also include information about how quickly they should expect to receive replies to emails, or how quickly they can set up a meeting should they need one. This way they'll understand that it's acceptable to expect a reply within 24 hours, rather than assume it's bad customer service if their email isn't answered within 30 seconds.

   As the call ends, your practice should confirm that the information will also be sent via email and will be in their inbox in a few moments.

Can you imagine the impact this will have? How it will leave your new client feeling?

And it doesn't stop there. You could pre-record a couple of videos on how they can maximise their results using your accounting firm and include these in a client area on your website, or email a link to them on YouTube. You can then drip-feed these videos over a few weeks or even months.

These first 100 days make or break a customer experience. As long as each correspondence provides value, there's no such thing as being in touch with a new customer too often.

## MAKING LIFE EASIER THROUGH AUTOMATION

During my time in the industry I've come across many apps that support delivery of an outstanding customer experience. There are cloud services and apps such as Xero and QuickBooks, or you can gather data using apps such as Receipt Bank and AutoEntry. There are hundreds and more are constantly being developed – which means there's simply no excuse not to leverage the technology that's available.

Practice Ignition is a business after my own heart. Its very core is a focus on helping accountants provide a great customer experience. Practice Ignition understands that customer satisfaction is an art form, and that a whole new industry has been built around this.

This is what Trent McLaren, Head of Accounting and Strategic Partnerships, had to say when I asked him about the platform:

*"Since we launched Practice Ignition and all throughout the years of development, we've always had our focus strongly on the client-adviser relationship, and automating the client on-boarding process really only scratched the surface of our ultimate goal.*

*You may see the signing of a proposal or contract as a necessary evil when first engaging with a new client, but this is a crucial point when it comes to building a strong working relationship with your clients."*

By making it easy to explain exactly which services you'll provide and what's included, Practice Ignition helps you to avoid "scope creep" and losing revenue on unbilled work. Focusing on a great on-boarding experience will make the process completely transparent and build trust

## MEET THE CLIENT WHERE THEY'RE AT

On average, people now spend over four hours a day – or about 86 hours a month – on their smartphones. Whether they're connecting with friends, shopping or keeping up to date with the news, smartphones are an integral part of our everyday lives.

If you want to provide exceptional customer service then you need to meet your clients where they hang out. Which means you need to be on their smartphones.

MyFirmsApp was one of the first companies to realise the power of accounting practices appearing on their clients' smartphones. That's why they created the opportunity for them to have their own app, thereby being ever-present in their clients' lives.

MyFirmsApp brings together a huge number of tools, and stores them in your own company-branded accounting practice app. It includes cloud accounting and client portals, and lateral thinking can open up other great opportunities. Many firms, for example, offer online diary booking, online payment, video channels, wealth management and more – all as modules inside their app.

## CLIENT-EXPERIENCE STRATEGY

When most firms think about their client experience they think about touchpoints – their individual transactions with prospects and clients. Whilst logical, however, this isn't the best way to approach a client-experience strategy. As business owners, what we really want is to create an end-to-end experience. In other words, only by looking at clients' experiences through their eyes, along the entire length of their journey, will we be able to improve their experience.

Client journeys include things that happen before, during and after they buy your services. These journeys can be long, take place across a multitude of channels and touchpoints, and last days, weeks or even years.

Whether you're bringing a client on-board, or want to deliver an excellent experience after they've signed up, a cohesive plan will ensure you maximise their experience.

Remember, you need to look at the client journey from their point of view. What are they looking for? (The Disney Compass Approach is a good starting point.)

Furthermore, providing a great experience doesn't start from the moment you sign up a client. It starts when they Google you and you're listed in the search results. Or when they read your Tweet or Facebook update, or see your website for the first time.

Every action your accounting practice takes is experienced by someone. Someone who'll evaluate – rationally – how you look and what you do, but also feel your vibe – emotionally.

## OPPORTUNITY IS HERE

For a long time accounting practices didn't need to invest in providing a great experience or to think like pioneers. However, times have changed and for a pioneering accounting practice opportunities are now everywhere.

That's why there's no better time to use the ideas I've outlined in this book if you want to be more visible, more vital, and more valued.

# TIME
# THE GREAT EQUALISER

At the beginning of every sales conversation, event, webinar and seminar that I hold, I ask attendees what their greatest challenge is. I've asked the question thousands of times now and the number one answer is always "time". Or, to be precise, the lack of it.

That's why I'm writing a few extra words around it. Time is the great equaliser for us all. No matter how rich we are, it's the one thing none of us can pay to get more of.

It's also why top business owners "chunk" their day. In other words, they block out certain times of the day to tackle different parts of their job. It means they can achieve everything they set out to do each day and prevents overwhelm.

In short, you need to create time in your diary for marketing. That way there's no getting away from it. Similarly, you need to block out time for your team, for meetings, for lunch, to actually do the work and, of course, for your family and friends.

Although each day has 24 hours, in reality only a handful can be used for marketing. I call these the golden hours. How you use them will ultimately decide on whether you fail, have average success or are a superstar.

By mastering time, you'll lower your stress levels and make more money.

## CASHFLOW FOLLOWS CALENDAR

If you show me your calendar and the actions you take every hour, day and week, I'll know where your priorities lie and be able to predict your cash flow.

Although every week effectively has 14 morning and afternoon slots, how many of these do you routinely set aside to work on the growth of your accounting practice? You spend time every day on your clients' businesses and on making their lives better, but how often do you spend time on your own business?

The moment I decided to set aside one or two of these slots to work on my business rather than in it, a shift took place. I no longer worried that I didn't have enough time. I'd scheduled time for it and it worked.

If I'd only ever scheduled time in my calendar for servicing my clients' businesses, eventually I'd have run out of clients. That's why you need to schedule time to work on your own business. Failure to do so will lead to the failure of your firm.

## 80% IS GOOD ENOUGH

Procrastination tends to kick in when you suffer from perfectionism.

And both are bad for business. Together, they create an infinite loop that destroys productivity and results. Perfectionism stems from feelings of insecurity around self-worth and hinges on what others expect of us. It's often referred to as the highest form of self-abuse because perfection simply doesn't exist. Even more importantly – unless you're a brain surgeon – it's rarely necessary in day-to-day life.

Once we realise that the expectations we place on ourselves are generally far higher than those that others place on us, we can relax a little. As I always teach my clients: 80% is good enough. And, even more importantly, 80% of "something" is better than 100% of "nothing".

So that blog post you don't think is quite right? If it's 80% right, publish it. The newsletter that still needs a couple of tweaks? If it's 80% there, send it. And those social media updates where you don't really know what to say? Start writing and press send.

Having a growth mindset and understanding that every marketing action you take is a learning experience will stand you in good stead here.

You need to be visible. An event with only 10 people will still help you build a community. A website missing a page will get more visitors than a website that isn't yet live.

Overcoming your perfectionism will stop you procrastinating and mean you get stuff done.

## THE 3% RULE

When I first started teaching social media strategies I didn't know anywhere near as much as I do now. In fact, I reckon I knew about 3% more than my clients. But 3% was enough.

As long as you know 3% more on a subject than your clients, you can help them. When it comes to offering advisory services, as long as you're able to read management reports and analyse the numbers better than your clients, you'll be able to advise them. If you understand how Xero works better than your clients do, you can advise them. And the same is true of all the platforms and Apps your firm uses.

The statistics and insights you've gleaned from this book mean that – compared to many of your clients – you now know 3% more than they do about marketing.

Never underestimate how much you already know. The 3% rule should empower you to teach and share your knowledge.

## BE THE PIONEER

If you're still running your firm the same way you always have, you're stunting its growth.

What's one definition of insanity? Doing the same thing over and over again but expecting the result to change.

In this book I've outlined nine key strategies to help you to do things differently.

The opportunity is there for you to apply these strategies in a way that's unique to your practice. If you do so, you'll not only change the way your clients see and experience your firm, but also the way they (and others) see the accounting profession as a whole.

It'll make you more visible, more vital and more valued. You'll have more time. Your team will be happier and your profits will be greater.

If you think this book is all about marketing, I'm sorry but you've missed the point.

It's about creating a life of freedom.

# ACKNOWLEDGEMENTS

I'd like to thank the hundreds of clients we work with at TwentyTwo Agency for showing up, playing full out and making a difference in the world.

I would like to thank Lucy Arterton, for without her sound advice and encouragement this book would still be just an idea in my head.

I would like to thank my darling husband and business partner, Matthew, for his unwavering support and cheerleading.

And finally thank you to my dear children Joshua and Annabelle, who have patiently waited for me to finish my book, and emerge from my office...

## NEXT STEPS

## FREE ONLINE TRAINING

Delve deeper into the nine strategies by joining me at our online workshop, The Pioneering Practice Blueprint

## LIVE EVENTS

Meet, mingle and engage with likeminded pioneering accounting practices that – by taking action – are reaping the rewards.

## COMMUNITIES

For free training, updates and real time inspiration, join the community at:
www.facebook.com/groups/MarketingForProfessionalAdvisors/

## THE PIONEERING PRACTICE PROGRAMME

If you would like to go into the nine strategies in greater depth, then I'd love to see you at one of our live Pioneering Practice Intensives: www.twentytwo.agency/live

Or, if you can't make it to a live event but are serious about growing your accounting practice, then we can talk about whether you'd be a good fit for our flagship Pioneering Practice Programme:
www.twentytwo.agency/pioneering-practice/

Completing a two-minute questionnaire by following the link above will automatically allow you to schedule a call for a ten-minute chat with us. During these ten minutes we'll be able to determine if we can help you or not. Using the information you provided in the questionnaire, together with what you tell us during the call, we'll help you to identify what's bothering you the most and provide three specific strategies to help you tackle it quickly.

The Pioneering Practice Programme is ideal for partners and business development managers of firms with an annual revenue of £150,000 to £5 million.

Find out more and apply today at:
**www.twentytwo.agency/pioneering-practice/**

I really hope I get to meet some of you soon – either at a workshop or in the programme. In the meantime, please do spread the word about this book and the website: **www.twentytwo.agency**.

Thank you so much for being part of my world and I wish you and your firm every success.

If there's ever anything I can do, just let me know!

## ABOUT THE AUTHOR

Amanda is one of the most highly respected and sought after marketing and branding trainers in the UK and around the globe.

Amanda was born in Brighton, and grew up in Croydon, South London. She now lives in Surrey with her Australian husband/business partner, her two children and her cat. From an early age Amanda has showed a passion for her life, and with determination and her unwavering belief, created a life of freedom.

Amanda is a multi-award-winning entrepreneur, business coach and marketing trainer. Her entrepreneurial journey started in 2009, and since the launch of her first business she has helped over 500 business owners start and exponentially grow their professional service based business.

Her entrepreneurial work has led her to become a mentor for Richard Branson's Virgin Start-Up Programme, speaking regularly on becoming a niche business, building a strong digital brand and webinar and event marketing.

She stands for living a passionate and freedom-based life.

If you would like to connect with Amanda, and find out more about her work, go to www.amandacwatts.com or connect with her on LinkedIn www.linkedin.com/in/amandacwatts

Dear Reader

If this book has helped you in any way (or even if you didn't enjoy it) I would be most grateful if you could hop on over to Amazon and write a review of the book.

If you then send a link or a screenshot to info@twentytwo.agency we will either send you free tickets to any upcoming events or gift you a free marketing training call (depending on where you are and what we have going on at the time).

Thank you, and I look forward to meeting you soon.

*Amanda C. Watts*

95386477R00109

Made in the USA
Columbia, SC
15 May 2018